"Just one thought is all it takes to alter the course of your destiny. One simple, yet profound thought that finds you right where you are, perhaps in a time and in a space in need of clarity, and it comes like light flooding a darkened space and leaving you with vision. That's what Tweet offers its readers in a thought-a-day format. But if you crave inspiration, you will not want to put it down."
Bishop Ray Mott, Generations Church

I personally came away from this experience a better, more confident person. My overall outlook and spirits lifted. I did not expect that result, but I wholeheartedly welcome it.
Jerry Reece, Author and co-founder of Reece Multimedia
Omega Nexus and Dark Beginnings

"Empowering and engaging; each anchoring affirmation draws you deeper and closer to a better you!"
Tanya Riggs, Real Estate Broker

Omar is brilliant by dropping daily nuggets that will inspire you in his new book "Tweet." Plug in each day for a thoughtful message to bless your life.
Dylan Raymond, Author of Rucksack to Briefcase, A transition Guide for Veterans and their families

Tweet 365 takes its readers on an insightful, year-long journey of exploration and contemplation. Written in a personal and guiding manner, Tweet 365 offers a creative approach to inspiration and reflection in easy to digest Small bites!
Dr. Hillary J. Knepper, M.P.A.
Professor, Pace University

"As a library administrator (and book lover) for over 30 years, I have seen and read countless books. Given my personal interest in self-improvement, I found TWEET to be both inspiring and practical. Omar Small's book provides daily lessons in helping people be their best selves. By using the wisdom of this book, I believe readers can improve and enhance the lives of themselves as well as family, friends, coworkers and the world at large. I highly recommend TWEET to individuals seeking to live better, kinder, and more successfully. "
Tom Geoffino

TWEET

365 Thought-Provoking Tweets to Ignite Your Brilliance and Power

OMAR T. SMALL

Published by Professional Standard Consulting LLC.
For inquiries and bookings, please contact:
info@brothersmalls.com
www.brothersmalls.com

Tweet: 365 Thought-Provoking Tweets to Ignite Your Brilliance and Power
Copyright© 2021 by Omar Small. All rights reserved.

Cover designed by Caleb Breakey and his team on Reedsy. All rights reserved.
Author photo by Aaron Kershaw

Scripture retrieved using www.biblegateway.com, operated by The Zondervan
Corporation, L.L.C.

**THE HOLY BIBLE, NEW INTERNATIONAL VERSION®, NIV® Copyright ©
1973, 1978, 1984, 2011 by Biblica, Inc.® Used by permission. All rights reserved
worldwide.**

Scripture taken from the New King James Version®. Copyright © 1982 by Thomas
Nelson. Used by permission. All rights reserved.

All rights reserved. No part of this publication may be reproduced or transmitted in
any form or by any means, electronic or mechanical, including photocopying,
recording or by any information storage and retrieval system, without the prior
permission in writing from the author, publisher and copyright holders.

ISBN 979-8-9853301-9-9

I want to thank my beautiful wife, Tonya Iris, for her love, encouragement, and support throughout the process. My three remarkable children, Noah, Caleb, and Sophia are an inspiration and remind me daily of the goodness, promise, and grace of God.

The content of this book is for information, education, and entertainment purposes only. Readers should not construe written material for personal or professional counseling, medical, legal, tax, financial and/or investment advice.

How to use this book....

Tweet is written to help you ask yourself questions, ponder possibilities, and move in a direction toward positive self-development and growth. We make decisions constantly, and understanding the components of decisions can aid in making choices for your ultimate benefit.

The UMASS/Dartmouth Effective Decision Making Process[1] prescribes that we first identify a decision needs to be made, gather relevant information, identify alternatives, weigh the evidence, choose among alternatives, take action, and review our decision and its consequences.

It sounds simple, but we know it's not that easy. Life is complex and complicated. Every peg does not fit snuggly into a square, diamond, or circle shape. There are nuances and unique circumstances we find ourselves grappling with. Some of these circumstances are due to our own decisions, and others are out of our control.

Whether you have control over a situation or you don't, the importance of honing your thinking skills through the decision-making process cannot be overstated.

Tweet is written in a way to help you become increasingly thoughtful, cultivating the inquisitiveness to dig deeper in recognition of your God- given brilliance. There are 365 distinct tweets/thoughts for your consideration including personal insights, prayers, lessons, reminders, encouragements, biblical references, and recollections.

My heartfelt desire is for you to become your very best and achieve your full potential. I believe when each of us tap into what makes us special, we all benefit and are encouraged to realize our collective ability for good. The process begins with one thought, one word, and one step.

There are several different ways to make the most out of this book. I encourage you to choose which way works best for you. Below are some suggestions—you may want to use one approach or combine them to meet your needs:

- Read a tweet a day for an entire year.
- Scan the book and read tweets that appeal to your personal interest and situation.
- Read the book cover to cover.

Whether you read the book cover to cover or read a tweet a day, please give some time and thought to each tweet. Think about and complete the questions, as they are designed for personal introspection and awareness.

Thank you for expecting, revealing, and sharing your greatness. It is an honor and privilege to partake of this moment and journey with you. Let's go!

Day 1

Good Morning. Do you realize the power in those words? Next level, new opportunity, another chance, recharge, revive, reveal more love, more life, get it right. So much value if you see it and appreciate it. So, I say to you from the depths of my heart, GOOD MORNING... You have been given an opportunity to participate in God's plan on Earth.

Life is a privilege and gift. In making that statement, I realize that many have endured much pain and suffering in their lives from abject neglect, abuse, mistreatment, poverty, deception, and discrimination. I acknowledge this world is laden with the weight of social ills, want, and misfortune.

I also acknowledge the world is pregnant with possibilities. That the Earth contains elements conducive to growth, development, freedom, prosperity, community, love, and peace. It is my responsibility as a citizen of heaven and a global representative to highlight and perpetuate that which builds and sustains life, wellness, freedom, good, and prosperity.

The morning represents the next step in your life's journey. The morning may represent solace from a trying ordeal. The morning may represent a do-over—I didn't do all I wanted to do or what I know to do, but I'm being afforded a second, third, and fourth chance to get it right and work on me...

My encouragement is for you to understand the power of "Good Morning." The power to do good today. The power to forgive and be forgiven. The power to say I love you. The power to share what is solely unique about who you are. It is my hope that you have a good morning!

Jot down three things you appreciate about morning time:
1.
2.
3.

Day 2

Consistency and excellence are intertwined. You must be consistent to be excellent. God's creation helps to better understand excellence: winter, spring, summer, fall, night and day, high tide and low tide, inhale and exhale. I want to be like God and be consistently excellent.

What makes a special performer, athlete, physician, artist, or chef? It is being consistently excellent. Think about your favorite restaurant. The food is always fresh and/or the service is impeccable. What would happen if it were hit or miss? Sometimes the food is really good and other times it is so-so or even poor. Not good, right? I think that is the definition of mediocrity.

Webster's Dictionary defines mediocre as of moderate or low quality, value, ability, or performance; ordinary, so-so. The fact is you are not designed to be mediocre. You were designed by an awesome and excellent God.

Is the sun mediocre? Is the ocean mediocre? Is the sky mediocre? Are the animals and birds? Are the variations of flowers and trees mediocre? No! These creations are amazing to behold. They are amazingly excellent because they operate within the confines of their nature. A bird flies, a whale swims, and a tree grows and produces fruit.

God created you and me in His image and His likeness to regulate over the creatures on the Earth. So, if we possess excellence, why do we find it hard to express that excellence consistently?

That question reminds me of a quote from the late great visionary Dr. Myles Munroe, "When you don't know the purpose of a thing, abuse or misuse is inevitable."

Any mechanic, physician, carpenter, or tradesperson will attest to the tools of the trade. A carpenter does not use a wrench to drill a hole. This truth seems to be apparent and considerably basic, however, we often go through the motions in life, not knowing our purpose and thereby wasting time, money, and energy. This is extremely frustrating to say the least. It is like putting your car in neutral with your foot on the gas. The neutral gear disengages all gears in the transmission and disconnects the transmission from the wheels. As much as you floor it, the car is inert. All that power and potential is untapped and underutilized.

Do you want to live your life in neutral and not reach your full potential or attain the goals you set for yourself?

Becoming excellent requires consistency. In what areas of your life can you be more consistent?

_____

_____

_____

Day 3

It is better to give than to receive. These words spoken by Jesus Christ help us to better understand His desire for us to be like Him. God is a giver, and everything that is good comes from Him. He wants us to be in the position to give.

In order to give, you have to be in a position to give. You cannot give what you do not possess. The mere fact you can give is a distinguishing characteristic and indication of your ability. Givers are in a blessed position, because very often they can share from their overflow or abundance.

If I bake a cake, I can share by cutting it in slices. If I own a car, I can give a friend or co-worker a lift. If I have a special skill or knowledge, I can share that knowledge with my family, friends, and community. If I am a compassionate person, I can share empathy with others. Being in the position of giver is where you want to be.

Think about what you have, your skills, abilities, attributes, and resources. Write down three things you possess that you can give or give more of.

1.

2.

3.

Day 4
When you look for opportunities to share and give love, you display the characteristics of God. Note: Sometimes love says no. Sometimes love is correction. Love tells the truth. Please do not equate love with co-signing everything. That is totally false and dangerous.

My nephew, Jonathan Alexander, is an amazing drummer, Instagram: Jonathan Alexander Drums. I would take care of him from time to time when he was a toddler. One such time, he walked around, or I should say stumbled around the house, as he was just getting good at walking. Unfortunately for Jonathan, he kept going toward the wall outlets, putting his hands on the walls and near the outlets. Several times I told him no and finally I had to pop him on his hand, No! He got the message—do not touch the electrical outlet.

This is a simple example of love being corrective. The same way love would warn you if you were heading into a ditch. I do not prescribe to the notion that everything goes, and everything is okay. Some things can be detrimental to your health and well-being, i.e., smoking, vaping, overeating, excessive drinking, and toxic relationships. Although you are free to partake in these activities, I would be less than loving if I did not encourage you to consider healthier choices. Have you ever displayed love to someone else by telling them the truth?

Has anyone told you the truth about an area in your life that needed adjusting? Have you taken their advice? Why or why not?
_____
_____
_____

Day 5
God's grace minus (-) your circumstance and situation equals (=) restoration, healing, peace, love, joy, prosperity, favor, salvation, order, hope, stability, clarity, vision, success, comfort, ability, capacity, wealth, health, wisdom, knowledge, understanding, forgiveness, acceptance, and purpose. Think about it.

Day 6

You got it. You got it (Affirmingly).
"It is of the Lord's mercies that we are not consumed, because his compassions fail not. They are new every morning: great is thy faithfulness."
Lamentations 3:22-23 (KJV)

As you approach today, recognize that God's mercy never comes to an end. Receive His overflowing and powerful grace in your life and let that knowledge permeate your thinking. You are loved.

Day 7

Looking forward to sharing with leaders...

I was recently asked to give the keynote address to recent graduates of a public administration master's degree program. My talk was titled the "Power of Authenticity." Some highlights of my speech are provided below:

<u>Your ability helps to deliver your authenticity.</u>

Authenticity is the quality of being authentic. Definitions of authentic are: 1. worthy of acceptance or belief as conforming to or based on fact. 2. not false or imitation; real, actual. 3. **true to one's own personality, spirit, or character.**

Former Secretary of State Rex Tillerson said, "Never lose sight of your most valuable asset, the most valuable asset you possess: your personal integrity."[2] Nicole Torres in a *Harvard Business Review* article[3] cited that feeling authentic at the office has been linked to higher engagement, higher workplace satisfaction, better performance, and better overall well-being.

I believe authenticity can facilitate diversity in the workplace as people bring their uniqueness, cultural and life experiences, personality, and skills to assignments and projects, providing a different perspective and viewpoint. Business to Business Marketing Strategist, James T. Noble put it this way: "Being authentic means staying true to who you are, what you do, and whom you serve. In an environment in which more human elements matter, it creates value and benefits for your followers as well as improving your business."

Some challenges to being authentic is our environment. It could be those close to you, co-workers, friends, or the media. We feel pressure to conform in ways that do not reflect our core values, or we find ourselves doing things that do not line up with our goals and aspirations.

To stay on track, it is imperative you find and foster your authenticity. Your loved ones can help in this regard. Parents, I believe, have a good understanding of what their children do well. I have provided some questions to help you pinpoint what authenticity means to you.

What is it that you do automatically? Something you do without thinking about it. Something that comes naturally to you. Something that you would do for free. Are you an exceptional listener? Are you always asking questions, perhaps with a desire to make things better or improve a process? Do you seek collaboration or bringing people/family together? Do you have a leaning toward establishing community? Ask a close friend what you do well.

Understanding and cultivating the qualities that make you unique is important to your career and personal advancement. Being authentic is something you can build on. Recognize it is the everyday change or contribution that will make the difference. Your ability, credentials, and stature help to deliver your authenticity. You take you wherever you go…If you are a kind, encouraging person who enjoys sharing and helping others, those personal characteristics will manifest in your relationships and occupation.

- **Authenticity helps you to build trust.** Establishing trust is key in relationships and facilitating change in organizations.

- **Authenticity allows you to spark the greatness in others and make a difference every day in other people's lives.** When you are authentic, you encourage others to be their authentic selves.

- **Authenticity helps to model the behavior and ethics you want in your family, organization, and business.**

- **Authenticity is a distinguishing factor that generates greater opportunities in your personal and professional life.** It highlights your uniqueness and makes you stand out.

I want to encourage you today that being authentic can catapult your career and magnify your personal and professional impact.

Describe personality traits that make you unique. For example. You are naturally curious, or you enjoy giving or teaching.

_____
_____
_____

In what ways can you accentuate and cultivate your personal traits in everyday life?

_____
_____
_____

Day 8

Did you ever consider that the proximity or position an individual has in your life is a glaring sign of the amount of love you are to dispense upon them? Think about it.

We do not choose our parents or where we grew up. We do not choose our siblings or family members. We oftentimes do not choose our neighbors. When you think about those closest to you, please consider they may be designed to draw something special out of you and vice versa. Cherish the moment and recognize the gift.

Day 9

Do not get stuck in cement. Recognize that daily learning is the mixture to cement your legacy.

After weeks of searching for a new job, I got an amazing opportunity. I started working and understood almost immediately that the position was not my final post. When I explained my position to friends and family, I would preface my statement by saying, I am not married to this position, I don't have my feet in cement.

One Sunday afternoon after church, I began to explain my position to Sister Vera. She listened intently, and when I said I am not in cement, she adjusted my perspective with the following statement: "What you're learning now is the mixture to cement your legacy (ability or capacity)."

Wow! Very simply, my thinking shifted. My experience on the job, in a new environment addressing new challenges would help cement my ability and capacity. It was something to embrace, realizing that my approach (attitude) to this new assignment and process would prepare me for the next opportunity and level in my life.

Can you think of a situation in your life that requires the right attitude to get the most out of it?

_____

_____

_____

Day 10

But God. That is the story of my life. The odds were stacked against me, But God. My mother and father divorced when I was about eight years old, and I can remember seeing my dad a handful of times after the separation.

As a child we moved a lot…so much so that when we obtained stable housing, I thought it was strange. I would anticipate us moving. We grew up in a two-building housing project in New Rochelle, New York, called the "Hollow." I saw fights, abuse, drug use, and hopelessness. Thankfully, my mother provided an awesome example of work, and she never let us feel less than. She raised all five of us as a single parent. Props, appreciation, and love for my momma and all the single mothers and fathers out there.

It is remarkable how time helps you to see more clearly. With age often comes maturity in that life has a way of teaching perspective through experiences. You understand friendship because you have had someone in your life who was trustworthy and someone who was not. Now you know the difference. You understand compassion because you may have had to be comforted or you had to support someone through a difficult time. You learned perseverance because you came through a very painful experience. You understand gratitude because you were taught the value of appreciation, or your experiences have instructed you that life does not come with guaranteed outcomes. We hope for the best, but sometimes we do not get it. Even in those times of disappointment, sadness, hurt, and pain, the right perspective can create the environment and conditions to springboard you into a better situation.

List two to three moments in your life that a positive perspective helped you through. If you do not have an example, write down a situation you are currently going through and the response or quality you desire to display through it. For example, I am going through a divorce…I hope to learn more about myself so I can be a better person.

_____

_____

_____

Day 11
Putting my debt on a bullseye target. Looking forward to hitting the mark over and over and over. Debt, you're going down.

How did we get here? Whether you owe hundreds or thousands, debt often creeps up on you, and before you know it, there is a mountain of debt before you. It's a constrictor like a boa, blocking and suffocating your vision and destiny. You are limited in what you can do because your resources are tied up. You would like to give more, but you can't. You would like to invest, but your savings are suspect. Well, we always have a choice. We made choices to get that dress, computer, or widescreen TV with surround sound. You had to have it? Or maybe you got carried away with the "holiday" season.

The weight of debt is not gained overnight. It is often the culmination of a series of decisions and lack of self-discipline. Now, there are situations in which credit is used for the bare necessities. Although understandable, the result is the same. The debt entraps you. What was touted as providing freedom (credit cards), does the exact opposite.

Okay, so you have debt. You are not alone, the average amount of debt by generation in 2020 was as follows:

- Gen Z (ages 18 to 23): $16,043

- Millennials (ages 24 to 39): $87,448

- Gen X (ages 40 to 55): $140,643

- Baby Boomers (ages 56 to 74): $97,290

- Silent Generation (ages 75 and above): $41,281[4]

Be honest with yourself. Recognize and assess where you are, then come up with a plan to get out of debt. You might need to reach out to a reputable financial advisor who will help you come up with a budget and plan to get out of debt. Make a quality decision to get out of debt and be forceful about it. The quicker you dismantle and destroy debt, the quicker you can take control of your life.

Create habits that align with your financial goals. Do you make enough money to support your lifestyle? Do you need to increase your earning potential and opportunities? Take an inventory of your spending habits and determine whether those habits draw you closer or further away from your goals. Being financially astute requires effort. I would say it's an everyday effort. Every day you must choose to be debt-free, healthy, and wealthy. No more putting your head in the sand or fantasizing about that deal or raise that will be a cure-all to your financial troubles. No! Decide to live your best life by being financially smart.

Write down three things you can do today to take control of your financial future.

1. _____

2. _____

3. _____

Share your goals with someone who can provide insight, guidance, and support by holding you accountable to putting your plan into action.

Day 12

If I or anyone says something and you take it, activate it, and use it, you are applying faith. It is not about me, rather it's the power God placed in you that is being tapped and honored. The principal is true, and I hope you make it work for you.

Write down one to three things you are going to work on today. I recommend you accomplish this task before you go on to the next day.

_____
_____
_____

How many days did it take you to accomplish this task? Now think about what your answer means as it relates to your focus. Okay, let's go!

Day 13

I recently received an award and thought to myself, I must do more, I must do more. I caught myself and said I must do me. I believe you are more impactful when you focus on uncovering the treasure inside of you. Your gift, once revealed, is for all of us to enjoy and benefit from.

A beautiful verse that illustrates this truth is found in Psalm 139:14 (NKJV). *"I will praise You, for I am fearfully and wonderfully made; Marvelous are Your works, And that my soul knows very well."*

Life is about discovering and learning. As you grasp knowledge, you realize how much you do not know. There are countless questions yet to be answered.

Life, through its peaks and valleys, helps to reveal who you are like nothing else. How many leaders were defined, in large part, by how they handled a situation or crisis?

I believe, as you learn about God through the Bible, you better understand your personal excellence, how wonderfully unique you are, and why you are breathing air right now. Doing you or focusing on what makes you unique is important to your growth and development.

What does doing you mean in your life?

_____

_____

_____

What behaviors/attributes do you need to possess and display in order to do you?

_____

_____

_____

Day 14
We must believe our future will be greater than our past.

Day 15
How infinite is the Most High God? The number of stars in the galaxy varies, assuming an average of 100 billion stars per galaxy totals about 1,000,000,000,000,000,000,000 (that's one billion trillion). [5]

Discovering this information brought fresh perspective to the following Scripture:
"He counts the number of the stars; He calls them all by name." Psalm 147:4 (NKJV). Think about it.

Day 16
When you appreciate the unfathomable greatness of God, you can better recognize the greatness in others.

Because I know God is awesome, unfathomable, all powerful, omnipresent, all-knowing, and sovereign, I can have joy and appreciate what He has deposited in you. There is enough of His glory and greatness for you, for me, and for everyone.

Day 17
Let out mean elevation.....flip it.

Instead of up and out, say out and up. Sometimes being out is preparation for going up another level. Shift your perspective.

Day 18
This year make a decision to talk to your elders.

Ask for and obtain their insight, knowledge, and wisdom. Peel away from the hustle, bustle, and noise of every day to honor them. Determine to learn from their examples and endeavor to pass it on.

Day 19
Brand new mercies. Brand new opportunities.

Every day when you open your eyes you have been afforded brand new mercies. You have another chance to love better, to grow, to learn, and shine. Take advantage of your gift and share it with the world.

Day 20
I'm standing...

Sometimes your stance is the victory. The ability or inability to stand is a characteristic and trait that defines your maturity in an area of life. It also impacts your self-esteem and helps to shape your legacy.

What I mean by stand is taking and holding a certain position or belief and displaying an upright attitude and posture in adverse conditions. Standing is your response to pressure, responsibilities, personal attacks, doubt, failure, mishaps, tragedy, mistreatment, loss, and life.

Character is tested in difficult times. Are you prepared and able to hold on until there is a breakthrough or release? History remembers the response of those like Nelson Mandela who persevered although the odds were against him. Your life and legacy will be determined by what you stand for and how you stand during trying times. We learn so much about ourselves based on the posture or stance we hold.

Is there an area in your life where you want to be resolute or unflinching? Please explain.

_____

_____

_____

Day 21
Should, Could, Would.

1. **Should** is a starting point where you have determined an action. I can climb this mountain. 2. **Could** is your confession and belief. I can do it. As you hike up. 3. **Would** is going down the mountain without reaching your goal. Keep moving onward 1,2,1,2,1,2,1,2,1,2, until you reach your destination. Don't give up!

Day 22
Young man, your stability will help her flourish and discover her superpowers. Young lady, your love and virtue will be a source of strength and confidence for him. Together there is no limit other than the ones you place upon yourselves.

How do you get there if the cycle/interaction described above is not evident in your relationship? Consider talking to a close and trusted friend who has been married for several years or seek personal and/or pastoral counseling. Good relationships are developed over time through seasons, circumstances, and challenges.

Day 23
Like searching for gold, you must dig to get the most out of this world and your life. C'mon, dig!

Day 24
Sobering but necessary: assessing your life and acknowledging your management or lack thereof.

Admit, "I did that." Do not stay there, take responsibility to change your position. Being honest with yourself is a step in the right direction.

Day 25

Thinking about what I will give my grandchildren...I have kids, but I realize the inheritance does not stop with them. Rather, it begins with them and must sustain for generations to come.

"A good man leaves an inheritance for his children's children." Proverbs 13:22 (NKJV)

We live in a society that promotes the individual. This book is dedicated to self-development. However, self-development and improvement should go beyond the individual and impact others. It is important we discover our ability and capacity, but it is equally important to recognize our discovery is for the betterment of someone else. Our families, communities, and our society are in desperate need of this ethic.

What are you determined to achieve or become? How will that achievement or realization benefit others?

_____

_____

_____

Day 26

"A man with health desires a thousand things, a man who is sick desires one."

-Confucius

Day 27

Let Him change you.

Faith is so important. A definition of faith is complete trust and confidence in someone or something. It can also denote your religious beliefs.

Hebrews 11:1(NKJV) reads, *"Now faith is the substance of things hoped for, the evidence of things not seen."*

I have heard the interaction between hope and faith explained this way by Pastor Ray Hadjstylianos of Living Word Christian Church: "Faith is the furnace or the capacity to reach the desired temperature, and hope is like the thermostat."

So, in this example, your hope being the thermostat, tells your faith, the furnace, your desired goal or temperature. One is not possible without the other, they work together.

A common phrase in church is, "Let Him change you." What this phrase means is to render yourself to God, submit to Him, and He will make you into the best version of yourself. I think it is a well-intentioned saying, but without explanation, it may be confusing. Initially, I thought about the phrase and thought, "I like myself." Others might have a notion that they will lose their very essence or the qualities that make them unique. I don't believe that God wants everyone to look the same or sound the same. That would be counter to his creation. Just look at the diversity in nature. No, I believe God wants to imprint those who acknowledge Him with His character and righteousness (His way of doing things).

I created www.brothersmalls.com to provide an example I don't believe is often presented in society. Many times, people of faith are characterized as boring, no fun, holier than thou, hypocritical, you name it. I wanted to send a different message that people of standard are real people with real struggles and challenges. We love, laugh, and hope. We dance, we enjoy our families, and earnestly desire to represent our faith in a way that gives glory to God. We are not spacey, but grounded and ready to be a positive force in the building of our families, communities, and world.

So, don't be put off by the phrase, "Let Him change you." Instead, realize everything in life is a process. As it relates to faith, a promise is found in Philippians 1:6 (NKJV): *"being confident of this very thing, that He who has begun a good work in you will complete it until the day of Jesus Christ."*

You develop as you spend time hearing words of encouragement, reading, speaking to others of like faith, and devotion. If you were learning a new language, it would be important to hear that language spoken often. A person who speaks fluently would not expect you to speak fluently when first learning the language. You would stumble with words and phrases. But if you stayed at it, sooner or later you would be able to communicate.

Some folks refrain from taking that first step because they feel they don't measure up or they'll be criticized. Whatever the endeavor, there is always a starting point. Please consider letting Him change you and know that He wants to present to the world the very reason why He created you.

If you would like God to reveal the best you, just repeat this prayer: God, help me to know you more and help me to understand my uniqueness and my purpose.

Day 28
When people say thanks a million, I receive it!

Day 29
I'm using you. Let it be positive.

Just spoke to some young people. I used names of people I personally know to encourage them.

Being perfectly honest, I will use the negative results as well, but as your friend, I would rather use the story of you overcoming. C'mon, let's go.

What am I saying? There is a lesson in everything. Life is loud with its pronouncements. All one must do is pay attention to gather insight and instruction. As a kid, I would see guys hanging out and drinking all times of the day and night. Now, I'm not against going out, hanging with friends, and having a good time. I think there is a time and place for that. But this was a daily occurrence for long periods of time. I would go to various places during the day, and when I returned, folks were in the same position.

As I watched their lives, I noticed many did not have successful relationships or careers, and many had serious battles with substance abuse and heavy drinking. For me, the lesson was clear:

- If you want those results/outcomes, take your place beside them.

- If you want something else for your life, then be mindful of how and with whom you spend your time.

I don't present this example to be mean or judgmental. In fact, people often accuse others of being judgmental. The fact is your decisions and actions judge you. If I eat ice cream, soda pop, and junk food every day and refrain from physical exercise, my actions will likely result in a poor health condition and disease. If I exhibit self-discipline, eat right, get exercise, and sufficient rest, then I'm more likely to have better health and prevent disease. Nothing to judge here, just the results of choices made.

So, as I teach young people to pay attention to the signs and pronouncements of life, I hope your personal example is one of positivity, of triumph, and victory. Whether it is good or bad, I will use it to learn and help those who have an ear to hear.

In the last year, what truth has life revealed to you loud and clear?

_____
_____
_____

Are you behaving differently based on your new understanding? Why or why not?

_____
_____
_____

Day 30
Don't be selfish. Don't hold back. Give us more of you. I encourage you to live on purpose today.

Day 31

If you know more, you can give more. Learn something new and expand your capacity to impact others in a positive way.

Truthfully, I am not the best with directions, however, if I travel somewhere, you will not have to tell me twice. If I see something, I take a mental picture and retrieve the information when needed. Although this visual way works for me, it does not help with providing directions.

When people ask for directions, I often think, I can take you there, but I can't tell you how to get there. I have to do better and learn directions so I can share them. In all seriousness, learn something new for your grandchildren. What you know now can impact generations to come. Pass it on.

Day 32

If you aim at nothing, you will hit nothing.

Day 33

You have what you can handle. If you desire more, show gratitude and appreciation by working and maximizing what you have to qualify for more.

Day 34

Use your superpowers for good and not evil.

Day 35

I have experienced things in my life that have made it clear that God has a greater design for my life.

When in high school, I had a very strange encounter with one of my basketball mentors. His name was FE FE Razor, and he could dribble, pass, and shoot the ball with the best of them. FE FE would knock on my door, and we would spend hours on the court, dribbling and playing one- on-one full court games. As a kid, I watched FE FE and other guys play ball, hoping to be picked. It was often late in the day when the court was available for me to get some practice in. I learned to get on the court early if I wanted to play.

Back in the day, guys played a full day of basketball, then retreated to smoke weed and drink 40-ounce bottles of brew. Unfortunately, this habit grew into a wicked addiction for some when other more destructive drugs were introduced, namely crack cocaine. As I grew and could show my prowess at developing basketball skills, those, including FE FE, whom I wanted to impress were caught up in an addiction more powerful than b-ball.

The court that once was filled with activity was now sparsely used. So many neighborhood ballers, instead of calling "next game," were consumed with getting their next hit. I avoided the after activity of getting high because I disliked how weed made me feel lackadaisical, and I was determined to work on my game. Also, to their credit, the older guys who were involved in this activity never approached me with it. That is why I found FE FE's actions so strange.

I entered the building's lobby when FE FE approached me aggressively, and grabbed me by my shirt. As he pulled me near him, he said, "Omar, if you ever do this (drugs), I'll kill you. If you ever do it, I'll kill you."

Nah FE FE, that's not me. Not sure where he got the notion, as I did not give any indication I wanted to use drugs or get involved with drugs. I had seen the destruction and pain it had caused so many in my community.

When I went upstairs, I began to think about what just happened. I actually was grateful for the occurrence. Here was a man who could not help himself, but cared enough for me to try and warn me to stay the hell away. This has happened to me more than once.

On another occasion, I was home from college and cut through another housing complex to visit family when a drug dealer quickly approached me. He opened his hand and tried to sell me crack cocaine. As quickly as he approached me, a drug addict who knew me came and stood between us, "Nah Man that's O, that's O. He's good." I kept moving, but as I walked, I began to ponder that this guy was offering me death. With that thought, I also considered the heroism of that addict, who came to my defense. Both instances were a clear indication of God's protection in my life.

Can you recall an instance in your life in which you could have gotten into trouble or were spared a consequence for your actions?

Recognize that others were not as fortunate and pay it forward by taking full advantage of your opportunity. Better yet, help someone steer clear of the same pitfall.

Day 36

When was the last time you were quiet enough to hear your own thoughts? Think about it.

Day 37

Relax, O. Relax. I found myself today trying too hard. You know, when you really want something. Be careful. You might be tempted to do things out of character. I caught myself today, and just had to say, "Chill out." God is my source anyway. What's for me is for me.

I had just finished reading a really good book and wanted to give an excellent review of it. That would be simple enough, but I also desired an interview with the author. So, I wrote in my book review that I wanted to interview the author on my website, www.brothersmalls.com.

Problem, most book review webpages are intuitive and do not allow URL's. I did not think about that initially. However, when I got a reply from the site with a request to revise my review, it became clear. So, what did I do? I attempted to convey the same information without using a URL.   I would like to interview Ms. Lynn on my show, "Kicking It with Brother Smalls" on YouTube. Well, I was not successful. Check out the message I received below.

You already submitted a review. Thanks!

Okay then. Getting this feedback was embarrassing. I immediately began to think, "O, Relax. You're trying too hard."

I know I am gifted, I know I have value, and I know that I would do an exceptional job given the opportunity to interview the author. With all that said, my anxiousness caused me to try to be too clever.

If it is going to happen, it will happen. I need to focus on my part, prepare myself, and keep plugging along. Furthermore, I did not do the author any favor because she received one less favorable review. This message was a reminder for me to continue to put my hope, aspirations, and dreams in God's hands by prayer, confession, and work. It was a reminder for me to recognize that all my success is due to His grace, mercy, and provision in my life.

Can you relate to this story? Have you ever acted out of character because you were so eager to make something happen?

_____
_____
_____

Day 38

What a difference a day makes. On the very next day. I got this communication:

Thanks for taking time to write a review. Below is a link to your review you can share.

Brother Smalls

☆☆☆☆☆ 5 out of 5 stars.

· 19 hours ago

Agent You Is A Must Read

Agent You is the best book I have read all year. It is chock-full of great advice. My book looks totally used with notes all through each chapter. I was truly conflicted reading the book, the questions and assignments are very thoughtful and useful. You want to pause to complete the questions, but you want to also forge ahead to finish the book. The content is fresh, and honest. Ms. Lynn reveals both her triumphs and her struggles in a way that is relatable, and real. I am going to take her advice and shoot my shot. I am looking forward to sitting down with her soon to discuss her book, life, and next level on my show "Kicking It with Brother Smalls" on YouTube. *Agent You* is a must read.

Day 39

Advance your growth and prosperity by humbling yourself. When you humble yourself, you display a willingness to learn and submit to a process of development. A humble student will ask questions, study, and complete assignments, facilitating a process by which good grades can be attained.

Humility is a key to elevation and success. What are you looking to achieve or accomplish? What acts of humility (habits) will aid you in reaching your goals?

_____

_____

_____

Day 40

Give today you, and it will be a great day!

Day 41

Be careful not to see the world through your hurt. We all have experienced pain. Realize you can convert pain into power/strength. Change your mindset, determine to get something good out of it, and determine to help someone through it. You will have begun to turn pain into power.

We often cover our hurts in ways that do not liberate us or protect the ones around us. When you are honest about your past, your struggles, and your pain, you lay a foundation for full recovery and restoration. Although that experience may always be with you, it does not have the same power over you.

As you share your story in a safe environment, you'll find that others may have had a similar experience. These individuals can be living examples of perseverance, providing encouragement for you to keep moving forward. Getting counsel from a trusted advisor, pastor, or therapist may be beneficial as well.

In dealing with matters of the heart, I have gained great solace, direction, and hope through reading and reciting scriptures, fellowship, church attendance, prayer, worship, and praise.

Romans 8:1-2, (NIV) states, "Therefore, there is now no condemnation for those who are in Christ Jesus, [2] because through Christ Jesus the law of the Spirit who gives life has set you free from the law of sin and death."

Sometimes when bad things happen to us, we find it hard to forgive ourselves. We beat ourselves up with woulda coulda shoulda. Stop it. Forgive yourself because if you trust in God, and confess your sins, you are forgiven by God, 1John 1:9.

When you actively implement these strategies, you are likely to experience greater strength, confidence, and freedom over time. Now, you can use your ability and knowledge to help and protect those around you. Your story can help others suffering in silence. Your story can also empower others with the knowledge to avoid the same pitfalls and negative situations. Salute! You will have turned pain into power.

Day 42

Gratitude. There are so many benefits to being grateful.

Here are three:
1. Gratitude grounds you. Helps you to observe your situation and realize others may have more challenges.

2. Fortifies you to see that you are fortunate.

3. Propels and qualifies you for more. Gratitude opens many doors.

What are you grateful for?

_____

_____

_____

Day 43

UNITED WE STAND, DIVIDED WE FALL.

Day 44

Word for the day:
Patience - The capacity to accept or tolerate delay, trouble, or suffering without getting angry or upset. There is a reason why it is a virtue. Patience is not easy, but necessary.

In what area do you need to exercise more patience?

_____

Why has patience been difficult in this area?

_____

_____

_____

What do you hope patience will develop in your life?

_____

_____

_____

Day 45

Why don't we do what we want? I encourage you to do the things you dream and think about. You can do it. Now do it.

What have you not done that you want to do? Why have you not taken steps to make it happen? Think about and determine three actions you will take in the next thirty days to accomplish your goals.

Today's Date:

List the three things you will do to accomplish your goals.

1.

2.

3.

Day 46

My grandfather would say, "Omar, when you complete a job, take a few steps back away from your work and see if you did a good job." He encouraged me to view things from a different angle to get a different perspective. This exercise can heighten awareness. Give it a try.

Day 47

Whether she runs or not, I am concerned about Ms. Richardson. I am going to pray for her and her family—that she becomes wiser, stronger, better, and more determined—that she realizes her full potential, and she continues to give God praise. Got you, Sis.

I wrote this after US Sprinter Sha'Carri Richardson was disqualified from participating in the 100 meters at the Tokyo Olympics after testing positive for a chemical found in marijuana. There was much talk of the rules being out of step with the times, however, marijuana is considered a performance enhancing drug by the World Anti-Doping Agency. Marijuana can relax athletes ahead of competition, which gives them a competitive edge and may enhance their performance. Whether you believe that or not, it was the rule prior to the Olympic trials. Ms. Richardson, to her credit, did not cast blame and took full responsibility for her actions.

Sha'Carri is fast, outspoken, and flamboyant. After the Olympics, she participated in a Diamond League Race at Hayward Field. The race was hyped, and there was much anticipation because the field would include the gold, silver, and bronze medalist sprinters from Jamaica, Ms. Elaine Thompson-Hera, Ms. Shelly-Ann Fraser-Pryce, and Ms. Shericka Jackson. The result of the race was resounding—the ladies from Jamaica again finished one, two, and three, proving they are in a class by themselves. Sha'Carri Richardson finished last and was more braggadocios in her post-race comments. After the race, she was vehemently ridiculed, and in my opinion it went beyond sport, and was mean-spirited, personal, and tribal.

Social media was ablaze with insults and derogatory memes. Some of the comments were even tribal in that it pitted one group against another. I honestly was put off by it all, especially comments made by those who know better. They added fuel to the fire. The fact is she got dusted, she came in last. No different than your favorite sports team getting blown out. It happens from time to time. One race does not make a career. In fact, I was inspired to coin this saying, "To become a champ, you have to spar with champions." How many boxers, performers, and professionals became elite because of their practice and proximity with greats in their field or industry? I believe this race will do more for Sha' Carri than many of her wins. That is my hope and prayer for her as a person, and an athlete.

When you perceive a "flaw" in someone else do you consider your own flaws? People need support, prayer, and guidance. Instead of talking about them, pray for them. How would you want someone to respond when you trip and fall? Think about it.

Day 48

Jesus had love for the hearer with every Word spoken. Imagine that. Whether it was words of compassion or words of correction, they were all assigned to deliver love to the hearer.

Your maturation in life is aided by your ability to hear and receive communication designed for your benefit. Sometimes we get caught up and distracted by how the message is delivered. We want it gift-wrapped with a bow on top. But sometimes the message is hard and abrupt. In these times we must be focused enough to distill the truth or lesson in the message for the benefit of our lives and those connected to us.

Can you think of a communication delivered to you that you have not implemented because of how it was conveyed?

_____

_____

_____

Do you know why you responded in the manner you did?

_____

_____

Do you want to respond in a different way in the future? If yes, please describe how.

_____

_____

_____

Day 49

Best decision I made in my life was to accept Jesus Christ as my personal Lord and Savior. Through Him all things are possible.

My faith has been integral in every area of my life. Applying for jobs, attending, and completing school, raising kids, and dealing with personal tragedies. The challenges and struggles of life can deplete and zap your hope. Watching the news can be depressing. We are bombarded with bad news and countless stories of people behaving in unimaginable ways. Faith helps you to see a brighter day, even when current conditions are unpleasant or gloomy.

What situation in your life do you need to exhibit increased faith?

_____

_____

_____

Do you have someone in your circle, a family member, a trusted friend, or a member of your faith community you can share this situation with? If so, please consider sharing the information and allowing them to pray with you, hold you accountable, and provide positive feedback and encouragement.

Day 50

Support for black and brown communities and support for law enforcement are not mutually exclusive.

Leaders should march in support of our law enforcement and communities of color who have often felt the brunt of discriminatory practices. In order to solve a problem, you must acknowledge that one exists and seek solutions that recognize disparities in justice.

I follow and support the Equal Justice Initiative. This organization, led by its founder Bryan Stevenson, works to end mass incarceration and excessive punishment in the United States, challenges racial and economic injustice, and seeks to protect the basic human rights for the most vulnerable people in American society. This principled and notable organization provides important facts of our past with the following assertion, "to overcome racial inequality, we must confront our history."[6]

Day 51
When life gives you homework, do it.

Day 52
Say yes today. Say yes to your potential. Say yes to your dreams. Say yes to your destiny. Say yes to your ability...Learn to say YES!

Day 53
Praying for someone other than yourself is very therapeutic. Try to make it a practice and habit. With a little effort you can find many causes to pray for. There is a lot of hurt in the world.

This is not just something nice to do but I believe it can support good mental health. Some postulate that being self-absorbed and excessively self-centered is a contributing factor to anxiety, depression, phobias, and a host of behavioral and anxiety disorders.[7] I believe this phenomenon is exacerbated by our virtual culture of seeking approval outside of oneself. Our social identities now linked to a keyboard and computer screen are depicted by our number of likes, friends, and followers.

Taking the focus off yourself and praying for others will help propel you toward action. Evidence shows that helping others can benefit our own mental health and well-being. For example, it can reduce stress, as well as improve mood, self-esteem, and happiness.[8]

Our young people need this ethic like never before. Please encourage those close to you to periodically take a break from posting, liking, and following to pray, volunteer, or contact someone who is isolated or do something kind. See examples below:

- Volunteer at soup kitchen.

- Call someone who is shut-in.

- Open the door for someone.

- Offer to carry the groceries or pay for a cup of coffee.

- Give a gift to someone who would not expect it.

These simple acts can be very encouraging for someone having a rough day, and chances are, you'll feel better in the process. Give it a try.

Day 54

"It is important to think on things that are good and reject negativity. A heart at peace gives life to the body." Proverbs 14:30 (NIV)

Day 55

Cowardice is real. We have real problems because often we lack the fortitude or courage in facing danger, pain, or difficulty. Be bold!

Day 56

Babies are messengers of hope. In their presence, the world seems brighter and full of possibilities. Let them speak to you. Smile and make it a great day.

When I was an administrator for a local municipality, the mayor would often ask an ice breaker question for the board members to start each televised board meeting. One night, the mayor asked the board and administration, what is your favorite smell? I think my answer surprised the group.

I unashamedly admitted I enjoyed the smell of babies. In the purest sense, they are simply little miracles from God that can bring unity. It is my hope people recognize and protect the unique gift and special opportunity that children bring to our families, communities, and world.

Day 57
A Social Context to Addressing Police Brutality

The work continues to address social issues including policing and our criminal justice system. We often take a myopic approach (near-sighted, lacking intellectual insight) to societal problems. When you have physical symptoms it very often indicates another issue in the body. The symptoms of poverty, crime, violence, domestic abuse, and discrimination must be viewed in a broader context.

As we look to create a world where all lives matter, we must focus on the root causes of our issues and work in every sphere to eradicate and destroy the components that lead to injustice, poverty, crime, neglect, and disease. Below is an illustration of a societal context to addressing police brutality, but it can be used to understand other social ills.

We have seen the difference of how policing is done in various communities. Why? Before we get up and put on our uniforms, we are who we are and come from an experience and context. We are the products of our conditioning. If you have been conditioned to view people as less than, violent, or criminals, then it very well may affect how you treat those individuals and police their communities.

I believe racism is a learned behavior built upon lies and bogus theories. That is why I am hopeful it can be eradicated if each industry and segment of our society seeks to identify and renounce racist theories and practices, and then actively promotes and institutes policies of diversity and equality. We did not get here overnight. We must acknowledge the history and vestiges of racial bigotry in this nation in order to reverse our course and save our country. We can do it. It is going to take all of us to make America greater.

Societal Context

Day 58
Treat resistance like weights to be lifted. It's exercise designed to make you stronger.

Sometimes the pressures of life may seem too much to bear. Sometimes with trying something new, you must climb over a mountain of doubt and fear. It feels like you are swimming upstream. Just recognize as you swim, as you climb, as you take steps, and hold your position under the weight, you are building the muscles, skills, aptitude, and attitude that will serve you well as you plateau to your next level in life. Treat resistance like weights to be lifted. It's exercise designed to make you stronger.

Day 59
I enjoy teaching because I love to learn. I always learn something from my students.

It was my first semester as an adjunct professor at the College of New Rochelle. I was recruited because the Department Chair Dr. Malcolm Oliver thought I had a great deal to offer. It started with a phone call. I received a call from students trying to complete a project in the master's in public administration program. I agreed to meet with the students. As the Deputy City Manager/HR Director of the seventh largest city in New York State, the opportunity to give back was an especially rewarding and gratifying part of the job.

I was informed that two students were waiting for me in the lobby. I invited them to my office, and they began to ask me questions about management. After the interview, one of the students said I should meet the chairperson of the graduate program. I agreed, and Dr. Oliver invited me to speak to one of his classes.

After the talk, I received great feedback and was offered an adjunct teaching position. I taught "Introduction to Public Administration, Public Policy, and Human Resources." It was a great experience, and I learned so much during the process.

Did the students gain? I think so, but I would say that I gained more. When you give, you qualify for more. The principle of reciprocity in business denotes the tendency that people want to give back something they receive. This need is strongest when the gift is given without expectation of return.[9]

I believe teaching is more akin to sowing and reaping. As much as you give, you get in return. The preparation, the dialogue, and feedback are an amazing process and cycle that truly defines a win-win scenario. So, seek new opportunities to learn and give. I believe, in return, you'll uplift others while building your personal capacity.

Day 60

I made a mistake today and caught myself. When I woke up this morning, the first thing I did was check Twitter. Y'all know that's out of order.

Day 61

I did it again. Yesterday, I woke up and social media got my attention. Today, I got up and it was chores and running errands. C'mon, O!

Day 62

It is super important we live life on purpose and in purpose.

Day 63

The Favor of God is amazing, outstanding, stupendous, extraordinary, mind-blowing, captivating, remarkable, fantastic, beautiful, incredible...

I will be back. Please add to the list.

_____

_____

_____

Great, good, awesome, best, ultimate, all encompassing, unforgettable, unwavering, consistent, warm, comforting, healing. Add some words of your own:

_____

_____

_____

There are not enough words to describe the goodness of God. However, it is an honorable and useful exercise to spend time and acknowledge how expansive the love of God is. So, spend a couple minutes reflecting on the goodness of God and how good He has been to you. Hint: If you are reading this book, you are blessed.

_____

_____

_____

Day 64

Love's in need of love today -Stevie Wonder

Good morn or evening friends
Here's your friendly announcer

I have serious news to pass on
To everybody
What I'm about to say
Could mean the world's disaster
Could change your joy and laughter
To tears and pain
It's that love's in need of love today

This song reminds me to be intentional about spreading love and hope. Listen to the song and determine how you can bring more love to the world. PEACE.

Day 65

I have the Greater One on the inside and bring excellence wherever I go. You are wonderfully made, and today your excellence is needed.

Day 66

I'm convinced my destiny is contingent upon my ability to acknowledge blessings in my life and render the appropriate care over them.

Day 67

A wise man once asked, "Do you want to impact the next corporation or the next generation?"

Women and men have done both, but when the rubber hits the road that is the question you have to ask yourself. For me, I will choose the next generation.
Sometimes it feels like society wants you to choose between your family and your career. Many are perplexed and stressed over trying to both climb the corporate ladder and find time to spend with their loved ones. It is not always an easy answer, but it is something that many couples and parents wrestle with.

If this is your situation, I pray you find the right answer and balance for you and your family. Think about it.

Day 68

God has invested everything in you. See yourself like He sees you. See yourself better, smarter, wiser, and stronger. See yourself blessed.

The concept of belief and vision are inextricably intertwined. If you have low self-esteem or a negative self-concept, chances are you'll see yourself that way and behave in counterproductive ways. The belief that I just described is defeating and often hinders you from getting started. You tell yourself why bother because you don't think you're worthy of good. The reverse is also true.

If you have a healthy self-worth or self-concept, then you'll likely see yourself as worthy of good, and you will act accordingly. This is why words are so important, especially the words you speak to yourself. *"And do not be conformed to this world, but be transformed by the renewing of your mind, that you may prove what is that good and acceptable and perfect will of God."* Romans 12:2 (NKJV)

What book, song, lesson/message has helped you to have a better self-concept?

_____
_____
_____

Day 69

God created the conditions, then created man. It was a planned process that took into account the environment necessary for growth and development.

He called forth light (day/night), divided heaven and earth, caused grass to grow, herbs, and trees with seeds within it to reproduce continually, sun and moon to regulate the day and night, fish in the sea, cattle, and creeping things on the earth, then man was created in the image and likeness of God. Because we were made in the image and likeness of God, we can create an atmosphere conducive for success.

If you think about nature, birds are meticulous in building their nests, and spiders are elaborate in weaving their webs. These are just two examples of creatures using the elements provided by God to create an atmosphere that is life-sustaining. You and I have that same ability. Before farmers plant crops, they cultivate the land, prepare, and fertilize the soil. School teachers return weeks before the start of school on a mission to prepare their classrooms to be learning hubs.

We don't choose where and to whom we are born, however, we have a choice to honor God by using the elements we've been provided to make life better for ourselves and others. When we approach our world from this perspective, we align ourselves with the design of God, and bring Him glory. Think about it.

Reference: Genesis 1-26 (NKJV)

Day 70

Increase joy, contentment, and happiness in your life by appreciating the little things…a ray of sunshine that warms your face, the fragrance of fall, feeling the breeze surround you as you breathe deeply, or enjoying the wonderment of a toddler…

What "little things" surround you that you can marvel in?

_____

_____

Day 71

I was born to reflect light, to shine, and to give and emanate love. My mission is to become brighter and brighter every day by the grace of God and help as many people as I can recognize that they, too, were born to shine brilliantly.

Day 72

Did you act or apply what God has instructed you to do? Your position as a parent is an awesome privilege and responsibility. Children also have a responsibility to listen and heed sound instruction and advice. That includes us as God's children. When we have completed the necessary coursework of study in school, we graduate to the next grade level. Similarly in life, when we apply what we know, we graduate from one level to another level.

Some jobs require you start at an entry-level position. To become a police chief you likely have to qualify by first becoming a police officer, than rise in rank and responsibility (sergeant, lieutenant, captain, deputy chief). It would be very strange for a police officer to rise in rank to police chief, especially if the position entails supervision over public safety personnel with a higher rank than police officer.

Our next level of graduation or success often depends on our ability to apply what we know.

What is the one and most important thing you know to do but are not doing?

_____

_____

Pray about it. Lord Jesus help me to:

_____

_____

_____

Day 73
It's not a game.

In late October and early November 2020, I noticed action from my fellow citizens that made me happy. Throughout the United States, people participated in democracy by voting. I am often up early walking my dog or exercising. I began to see people gather at polling sites with folding chairs, blankets, and other supplies hours before the polls opened.

One Saturday morning, I walked my dog around eight forty-five. I saw a line start to form and thought perhaps I could do my civic duty, anticipating the polls would open at nine o'clock. When I asked a gentleman in line what time the polls opened, he said, "Noon."

On a Saturday morning people began to get their spots some three hours before the polls opened. It fascinated me that it was not a sporting event or a concert or some new version of a popular gadget that people lined up for. No, people waited in line to ensure their voices were heard. I did not care about who folks voted for as much as the participation I witnessed.

Day after day, in nice and inclement weather, Americans lined up to cast their vote. Many experts predicted an historic turnout. Prior to the election, Professor Michael McDonald of the University of Florida stated it was possible that more than 160 million people would turn out to vote.[10] His prediction was spot on. According to Pew Research there were approximately 158.4 million people who cast their vote on Election Day.[11]

This election was historic in many ways. Moving forward, my hope is that all Americans, no matter their political affiliation, adhere to something we espouse and teach our children:
I pledge allegiance to the flag of the United States of America, And to the republic for which it stands, One nation under God, indivisible, with liberty and justice for all.

Day 74

Drivers, start your engines has been a call before many car races.
It is a moment before the race starts when all competing racers turn on
the ignition to their vehicles. Each contestant will end the race at
various times and positions. In life so will we. Stay on your track.

Day 75

*Peace. I speak peace to you. May the peace of God envelope your
heart and mind today. May you cast your cares upon Him, for He
cares for you. May you realize, acknowledge, and know without a
shadow of a doubt that He will never leave nor abandon you...exhale.*

Day 76

*The knowledge of God is so vital to your development and growth, it
cannot be overstated.*

When you lack knowledge, you are more susceptible to the dictates of
those who do not have your best interest at heart. There are many
voices we are bombarded with on a daily basis. These voices come
from the media, commercial ads, internet, societal agencies, and other
people including your friends and family members. As you attend to
these voices, it is paramount you are equipped with the truth to
determine whether you will heed their suggestions or cast them aside.

Many people live with lies about themselves. For example, our society
often portrays one body type over another as it relates to beauty. If
people don't know the truth that they were made wonderfully by God
with extreme care and consideration, they may develop a "less than"
mentality. This mentality or low self-worth may manifest itself in the
choices they make about their career, relationships, and overall
outlook. I repeat, don't fall for the trick. Get the truth and hold on to it
for dear life.

Day 77

You've got to know who U are & learn to LOVE who U are.

"Not 1 drop of my self-worth depends on your acceptance of me."
                                    – Quincy Jones and Ray Charles

Day 78
How long?

Many times in life we ask the question, how long? How long until I get my breakthrough, my opportunity, my healing, and restoration. It's frustrating. It's tiresome, but don't give up now. You've come too far.

Continue to work and pray. Continue to believe, trust, and confess that your next level is closer than it was before. Praise God because the joy of the Lord is your strength. You can do it, just a little while longer.

Love, grace, and peace, family.

Day 79
I own the most expensive and expansive computer in the world, and you do, too. It is called your brain. In 2016, a scientific research study suggested that a human brain may be able to hold as much information in its memory as is contained on the entire Internet.[12]

Question is, what will you program it to do? Love, attain wealth, speak life, make healthy choices, choose healing thoughts, see greater possibilities, and obtain solutions? What do you think?

Day 80
You only live once, dude.

I was talking to my friend and workout partner, Fire Chief Andy Sandor. I told him about my plans to resign a very prominent position and pursue my dreams of entrepreneurship and writing. Before I finished speaking, his response was straight and to the point, "You only live once, dude."

Is there something you are holding back on? A dream, a business, a vocation that you have always wanted to pursue. If this describes you, I will encourage you just as Chief Sandor encouraged me. "You only live once."

Spend time writing down your thoughts, pray about it, and make a plan. Then speak to someone you trust about that plan and fine-tune it. Once you have a direction or vision, determine to study it, obtain additional information, and begin to pursue it. You will likely need to refine the plan and make adjustments along the way, but as you move closer and closer to it, the vision/goal will become clearer and clearer.

Write down two things you have always wanted to do.

1.

2.

Spend time thinking about how you can move closer to doing the things you have always wanted to do.

Day 81
I find delight in saying yes and no.

Day 82
Anytime we love, give, plan, and pursue that plan we demonstrate Godliness.

"For God so loved the World that He gave his only begotten Son, so whosoever believes on Him would not perish, but have everlasting life." John 3:16 (NKJV)

When we encourage, uplift, celebrate life, and help to restore, we exhibit God's goodness.

"Let your light so shine before men, that they may see your good works and glorify your Father in heaven." Matthew 5:16 (NKJV)

How do people know what you are about or what you represent?

_____

_____

_____

Day 83
You were born to produce. Question is, what are you producing?

Day 84

Sing your song. As I read this morning. I remembered a song and began to sing. I encourage you today to sing your song and be refreshed...Good morning!

P.S. I will share mine if you share yours...Let me know at info@brothersmalls.com under the Subject: This is my song. Please share the name of the artist and a sentence or two on how the song makes you feel or how the song helps you.

Day 85

Managing money helps in so many areas in life. I believe managing money helps to order your life. There is a peace that comes when you set things in order financially.

Day 86

What do you want out of life? What are you putting into it?

Determine to put into your relationships, businesses, family, and health, your desired outcome. Go for it.

Day 87

Are we there yet?

The cute and sometimes annoying phrase that kids exclaim on road trips. Honestly, it is the right response. Children do not plan road trips, nor do they understand the route. They are dependent on the adults, and thus the question is appropriate. I think we need to recognize the brilliance in that question. Do we know how far we must go? In many instances, the answer is no. How much gas is left in the tank? How much money is the account? How is your overall health? Where are you in pursuit of your goals? Are you there yet? Understanding where you are is important to getting to where you want to be.

Day 88

Why is it important to renew your mind daily?

Just turn on the TV or listen to the news. There is a design that would have you doubt, live in fear, and forsake your God-given promise and destiny. That is why you have to take action each day to sow seeds of health, stability, prosperity, charity and community.

Listen to a positive teaching or some good music, focus and count the blessings in your life. Read a book. Talk with someone you respect. Pray and chart a new direction and course for your life. Just be deliberate to protect yourself and your family from an onslaught of negativity. I PRAY YOUR PEACE.

Day 89
All dogs go to heaven.

When we brought him home, we could carry him in one hand. That changed rapidly as he grew into his big feet and floppy ears. Blaze, our strong, loyal, and handsome 120-pound African Lion Hound, aka Rhodesian Ridgeback.

People would stop me and gush over how impressive he looked. What happened to him? Some thought the line down his back was a scar. I explained that breed has a unique characteristic. The hair on their backs grows in the opposite direction.

When he got excited, the hair on his back would rise and resemble a Mohawk haircut. Blaze loved the attention, and I was a proud owner. I didn't mind telling strangers about the breed's history of hunting lions in packs of three. The term "keep a lion at bay" came from these dogs. They were athletic enough to run with a hunter on horseback for up to thirty miles and brave enough to chase after and distract lions while their masters took several shots at the big cat.

Blaze was a perfect family dog. He was good with anyone we invited into our home. You had to be invited 😊. Everyone in the house had a special relationship with him. He was my workout partner.

Shortly after I got him, I got a health report that required me to pay better attention to my overall health. He helped me to get in shape. I walked and ran him everywhere. The next visit to the doctor's office was much more enjoyable. My cholesterol levels were lower, and I had lost seven pounds.

If you own a dog, you know how they can relieve stress. No matter what my day was like, he lavished me with unconditional love. When I opened the door, he was there wagging his tail to greet me. When I needed to take a break, he provided that, too. "Babe I'm going to walk the dog." Getting out with him rejuvenated me. I was able to collect my thoughts, relax, get away, and process the day.

Three years ago, Blaze gave us a scare. He lost twenty pounds, was lethargic, not eating, and dehydrated. I was concerned he ate or ingested something during our walks. During the spring/summer months, herbicides and lawn care chemicals are used a lot, and dogs are always sniffing around. In my mind I thought he ingested the residue of a lawn care product or consumed something that did not agree with him. After several trips to the vet and some antibiotics, he rebounded and gained all the weight back, disaster averted.

This week, he exhibited the same symptoms. I thought to myself we'll institute the same protocol. Get him hydrated by any means including using a turkey baster to spray water in his mouth, get him to eat something including baby food and boiled chicken and rice. These remedies did not work, he could not keep anything down. Blaze got weaker and weaker day by day. We scheduled an appointment for the next day, but that night his condition dropped precipitously. I heard him moaning in pain around four o'clock in the morning, and I knew we had to rush him to the emergency room (ER).

My son and I carried him to the car, as he was not able to walk on his own. We were on the road, calling around to find an ER that was open. The first two animal hospitals we contacted were either closed for the night or filled to capacity. We finally found one that would receive him. When Blaze was diagnosed, the doctor said his condition was critical. When she returned, the news got worse. She explained, if my dog was a human, he would need dialysis. Blaze was in kidney failure with a heartrate of 190 beats per minute. He was in excruciating pain and laboring. My wife and I made the decision to put him up. I say put him up instead of putting him down because I believe **all dogs go to heaven**.

It was seven-thirty, and we had to race home because I had a conference for work. My wife and I decided to keep the news about Blaze until the evening so the kids could have a productive school day. That evening we huddled together in the living room and explained the condition Blaze was in and the report from the veterinarian. We told them Blaze had died. We cried as a family and consoled one another. It was a very sad time, but I had mixed emotions. Along with sadness, I had a lot of gratitude, thankful God gave us such a wonderful creature. I was thankful we got three extra years of companionship and joy. I was grateful our family came together to pay tribute to our four-legged friend and beloved family member. We all received condolences from friends and loved ones.

As a father, teacher, and leader in my home, I cherished the example being set. Blaze, in his life and death, taught us about the cycle of life— how we need to love and appreciate one another every day because life is not guaranteed. Some people, after a loss of a pet, vow never to get another one. I can certainly understand this sentiment, but that will not be our approach. We will always remember Blaze; he was one of a kind. With that said, when the time is right, we will again bring dogs into our home to share love and new experiences. What a special gift and amazing opportunity.

All the emotions, tears, laughter, care, and stories we shared were all due to Blaze. These displays of love, I believe, makes God smile. Think about it. If man is made in the image and likeness of God, and dogs are "man's best friend," then I would think there is a special relationship and love the Father has for these beautiful creatures. Dogs have cemented their place in our homes and hearts by giving unconditional love, loyalty, and companionship. So, call me soft or whatever, if you ever cared for a dog, I think you would agree that **all dogs go to heaven**.

Day 90
To whom much is given, much is required. Luke 12:48 (NKJV).

The amount you are allotted does not diminish your responsibility to care for and cultivate the gifts provided. Whether you have a large house, small house, or apartment, the rooms require cleaning.

Day 91
I did not get the approval of a father, but God provides.

I have two older brothers. Their approval or disapproval was significant in my formative years. In fact, just recently my oldest brother Al congratulated me on an interview. "Good job, O! Excellent work." It felt amazing.

I recall a time when my older brother Marc came to see me in college. We visited a nearby university. During the night there was a fire alarm, and after a few drinks, I was goofing off and acting foolishly. My brother, Marc, who, in my opinion, was the party animal of the family, looked at me disapprovingly and said, "O, you buggin." Those three words snapped me out of my stupor. It was like he verbally slapped me in the face. In retrospect, he may have been peeping into how others were checking me out while I acted silly. In any event, his words hit the target. I immediately changed my behavior and got myself together.

Please remember:
There is a sister, brother, friend, mother, father, neighbor, or kid in the neighborhood who needs your voice of approval or correction. Do not discount the power of your voice. Use it to positively impact the lives of others in your family and community.

Day 92
COVID-19. Felt great to be in church on Sunday.

A little different with the protocols and distancing, but just as impactful. Y'all try it out.

"I was glad when they said unto me, let us go to the house of the Lord." Psalm 122:1 (KJV)

I had a conversation with friend who is a lawyer. He told me that an individual he was talking to at the courthouse lamented about the impact of COVID-19. Prior to the pandemic, this individual was able to visit a church when he needed a lift without registering beforehand. Many churches have not opened their doors for in-person services, and this has created a real void for many people. During this time, believers must be deliberate in reaching out to others.

Day 93

I have no good reason not to succeed. Christ paid it all. My job is to give thanks and acknowledge the promise daily.

Day 94

Did you ever consider that the thing that bothers you most about our world, is the thing you are designed to address?

Is there an issue in society that captivates your interests or causes you to get upset? Write down three issues below.

1. _____

2. _____

3. _____

If you could only address one issue listed above, which one would it be?   Why?

_____

Answering these questions will help you discover your motivation, passion, and purpose. Now that you have a better understanding of your motivation, investigate ways you can make a difference. Many causes have been the impetus for establishing foundations and nonprofits.

Discover how you want to support the cause and make this world a better place today. THANK YOU.

Day 95

Sometimes you can please God and Man. Other times you have one choice. Think about it.

Day 96
Acknowledging God helps you to perceive good, to see good.

Vision and perspective is super important to detecting the possibilities and opportunities in your life. Acknowledging God helps with a heightened sense of appreciation and gratitude. Now that you recognize and appreciate how fortunate you are, you can see the finish line. Your goal is in sight. Catch your second wind, put it in gear, and finish strong.

Day 97
Listening and following directions, an important skill.

If I gave you directions for a recipe, process, or destination, you would need to listen and follow the directions to ensure success. Important is our ability to hear and comprehend correctly. Doing so, lessens costly and timely mistakes.

Endeavor to hear right. Then act on what you know. Your action is necessary to become skillful. You have to hear and do.

Reference: James 1:22-25 (NKJV)

Day 98
Think about your circle. Think about your life. Think about your world. Is there a cause to pray?

Day 99
"The greatest deficit in our cities is never money, space, or ideas; the greatest deficit is trust."
– Bishop Dr. Redford Mott

Day 100
It's spring! Although the weather is unseasonably cold, I have determined to enjoy the outdoors. Sometimes you must spring into your next level regardless of what it looks like outside.

Words related to spring—arise, originate, derive, flow, issue, emanate, proceed, stem. Quite possibly there is something that seems delayed in your life.

Spring into it.

Day 101

Real love and devotion are possible, but it will take work, a true commitment. A key is to find someone who is willing to work with you.

Prayer: God give me someone who will trust you and work each day to make heaven on Earth. ♥ 👐 🙏 ♥

Day 102

"He will win who knows when to fight and when not to fight."
– Sun Tzu, The Art of War

If you were trekking in remote woods or the jungle, you would equip yourself with materials and information to give yourself the best chance for survival. In the same way, people of color need to be equipped to handle challenges we may face. It is unjust and unfair that I and other people of color have a different set of rules as it relates to encounters with police.

A close friend and I had an unprovoked encounter with police in college. We were simply walking down the street in broad daylight when the cops drove their car on the sidewalk and drew their guns. We did exactly what we were taught by our parents and community elders, and thankfully we are here to tell the story.

In the past, Blacks have had to travel on certain roads at certain times to increase their chances of a safe passage. This sucks, however, it is true and a part of this nation's history and sin.

I advocate we continue to fight and demand justice. We should also remind each other of the materials and information that will increase our chances of surviving encounters with the police.

1. Dashboard camera.
2. Traffic stop. Pull over in a well-lit area if possible.
3. Hands on the steering wheel.
4. Look at officers and ask questions and/or repeat commands slowly and deliberately.
5. When complying with commands, tell officers exactly what you are doing.

PLEASE STAY ALERT AND COMPLY
TO THE BEST OF YOUR ABILITY.

I present this list to give our folks the best chance to survive encounters. I do not consider it being a punk. I am a grown man with a family, future, and destiny. We have all witnessed people complying fully and still being victimized. Our forefathers had to do this and much more in order for us to be here today.

Other suggestions:
- If a ticket was given erroneously, fight it in court.

- If you were treated unlawfully, unfairly, or discriminated against, lawyer up. Fight it in court and require restitution $$$.

- Train others to equip themselves with materials and information to increase their chances of survival.

AS WE FIGHT THIS BATTLE, LET'S BE STRATEGIC ON WHEN, WHERE, AND HOW WE ENGAGE THE ENEMY (discrimination, hatred, conscious and unconscious bias, and all forms of injustice).

"He will win who knows when to fight and when not to fight."
– Sun Tzu, The Art of War

Day 103
A good word has the power to lift you out of depression. We all get down at times. Bad news, physical ailments, lack, stress, and anxiety can all contribute to it. But...

The good news is: a good word can provide a refreshing, hope, and a new perspective.

Encourage yourself.

You've got to eat your vegetables. Vegetables are good for your body and provide the necessary nutrients and vitamins for your body to thrive. Similarly, positive, and instructive words are good for your mind and personal development.

You must have a healthy diet of both good food and good words. Do you? Take time to reflect and share your thoughts below.

_____
_____
_____

Day 104

When I was growing up, the guys in the neighborhood use to call me Smalls or Brother Smalls. I am so grateful that I am known by that name.

It means a lot that people confide in me, sharing their hopes, dreams, and challenges. Then they allow me to speak into their lives. As I grew, the name fit my lifestyle and outlook. I learned to better appreciate different perspectives by listening intently to others and paying attention to my environment.

It is with earnest desire and great appreciation for learning that I share with you "Kicking It with Brother Smalls," at www.brothersmalls.com. This website features vibrant talks and interviews with artists, entertainers, business and civic leaders, teachers, and everyday people with something to contribute to our world. Subjects include love, relationships, music, entertainment, business, sports, historical, current events, and more.

Day 105

Walking down the street, a lady said to me, "You're looking damn good." I told her thank you and kept walking.

When I was a youngster and my grandfather took me to get a haircut, he would always say, "Omar, you look good, but you got to be good." Thanks, Grandpa. Our society puts a premium on the outer appearance. This is a proven fact when you consider that cosmetics and beauty supplies make up (no pun intended) a multi-billion dollar industry. Have you ever noticed how someone who is inwardly an amazingly, beautiful person has a great attitude and pleasant disposition? Just being in their presence makes you feel different. You feel good around them. In contrast, have you ever been around someone who had outward beauty, but inwardly they were lacking? They lacked substance, depth, empathy, and warmth. Their focus was disproportionately on their outer appearance.

God said man looks on the outer appearance, but He is concerned with the heart or inner self. He instructs us to not have beauty only in the outer appearance, but more importantly, let it be the inner person. Let beauty come from the inside out.

References: 1 Samuel 16:7, 1 Peter 3:3

Day 106
One more day.

One more day closer to graduation. One more day closer to your goal. One more day to discover how uniquely special you are. One more day to say I love you and to receive love. One more day to give a hug. One more day to learn something new.

What will you do today?

In a published article of "National Geographic," it was suggested that after centuries of effort, some 86 percent of Earth's species have yet to be fully described. According to the study, our planet is home to 8.7 million species. [13]

One more day closer to seeing my Lord and Savior face to face. I recognize His creation and I appreciate you more than you know. I also understand that I am passing through this life, which is why I am compelled to touch others with the life given to me.

Day 107

Listen.

Your ability to hear is important to your ability to receive. As you apply what you have heard, you qualify to hear more and more.
Reference: Mark 4:24

Day 108

Moving the meter today. Here a little, there a little. Make it happen, people. Make every day count by doing something to move closer to your goals.

Day 109

See obstacles. See opportunities.

Day 110

Omar – Eloquent (gifted speaker). Strong. Rock. Sharp. I want to thank my mother and father for giving me my name.

I often ask people I meet what is the meaning of their name. Some may think that question intrusive, but I think a name provides information on the type of person you are or can be.

Hint: If your name is unique in that there is no known definition, you are quite fortunate. Choose your most positive attributes, and add some words you want associated with your name. Attach those words to your name and repeat it to yourself over and over again.

If your name does not have a positive meaning, keep searching. There are many different definitions for names and words. Accept the positive and reject the negative.

Note: *"A good name is rather to be chosen than great riches, and loving favour rather than silver and gold."* Proverbs 22:1 (KJV)

What is the meaning of your name?

Does your name describe you in any way?

What words do you want associated with your name?

Think about it.

Day 111

If you are looking for something (action and intent), you are likely to find it.

What are you looking for? What are you pursuing? Perhaps the answer lies within the search.

Day 112

When someone transitions from this life to the next, we who remain consider the impact and impression those who have gone before us have made.

The outpouring of tributes to luminaries like Cicely Tyson, John Lewis, Diahann Carroll, Jackie Robinson, and many others denotes their essence, dignity, and character. We are blessed to have witnessed their greatness.

Have you ever thought about what people will say about you when you make your transition?

We should think about this more often. It will help us to be focused on the next generation, and the legacy and path we are leaving them. I submit to you that the individuals I named above thought about you and me and acted accordingly.

Day 113

I asked a good friend, "How are you doing?"
He replied, "I keep going."
I encourage you today, keep going.

Day 114

We have so many stories to tell.

I'm tired of the same stories being told through movies and TV shows. Drug kingpin wannabe, etc. Can we give it a beat? If there is no redeeming quality to it, I'm not interested. Make a conscious effort to support work that highlights the broader range of our experiences.

The list below is not exhaustive, but represents shows I could comfortably enjoy with the entire family. Please add to the list.

- "Cosby Show"

- "A Different World"

- "Little House on the Prairie"

- "Living Single"

- "Roc"

- "The Wonder Years"

- "The Jeffersons"

- "Family Matters"

- "Fresh Prince of Bel-Air"

- "Parenthood"

- "Everybody Hates Chris"

- "Sister, Sister"

- "The Brady Bunch"

- "Sanford and Son"

- "Gilligan's Island"

- "Amen "

- "Steve Harvey Show"

- "In Living Color"

- "Good Times"

Day 115

My grandfather used to say, "It is a full-time job minding your own business." He could only imagine the distractions we now deal with.

It takes work and determination to stay focused. How many times have you set out to do something, and before you get started, you are doing something totally different? Before you know it, the day is spent, and you have not accomplished anything remotely related to what you set out to do.

Be encouraged. We often have starts and stops. The key is to keep your momentum and not get discouraged. Just know that it takes work.

"Above all else, guard your heart (mind), for everything you do flows from it." Proverbs 4:23 (NIV)

Day 116

It is easier to build strong children than to repair broken men."
– Frederick Douglass

What can you do to invest in the next generation?

Day 117

Been through a lot to give a lot. What does that simple phrase mean to you?

_____

_____

_____

Day 118

You are proof of process.

Time and change happen to us all. We look and perhaps think differently than we did a year ago. Everything in life is a process. Although we fantasize about change in a blink of an eye or snap of the finger, change rarely ever happens this way. Think about it. The tree you see in the winter does not look the same in the spring. It goes through a process of regeneration that takes many days and weeks to complete.

Your development and achievement in life is a process aided by the action steps you take every day.

Day 119

"Make a joyful shout to God, all the earth! Sing out the honor of His name; Make His praise glorious." Psalm 66: 1-2 (NKJV)

We honor God by acknowledging His awesome works.

Hint: Just look outside or look in the mirror. Feel your heartbeat or listen to the sound of your voice. You are amazing!

MORNING PRAYER

Day 120

A prayer in six parts, (Part 1).

Our God, we come to give You praise and to honor. Lord, You are our sufficiency, You are everything we need, the lover of our souls. You are our hope, and in You, Lord Jesus, we put our trust. You are our way maker. We elevate Your name which is above every name. We elevate Your work on Calvary to the saving of souls, and we elevate Your promise of life and that more abundantly.

Day 121

Morning Prayer (Part 2)

You are our strong tower, our battle ax; For the weapons of our warfare are not carnal but mighty in God for pulling down strongholds, [5] casting down arguments and every high thing that exalts itself against the knowledge of God, bringing every thought into captivity to the obedience of Christ, [6] and being ready to punish all disobedience when your obedience is fulfilled."

References: Proverbs 18:10 (NKJV), 2 Corinthians 10:4 (NKJV)

Day 122
Morning Prayer (Part 3)

As a church body, we agree this morning in Jesus' name and are assured what we ask for will be done by our Father in heaven.

We come against the spirit of premature death in Jesus' name. We say be removed and be cast into the sea. We rebuke and cancel death, diabetes, heart attacks, high blood pressure, confusion, chaos, hopelessness, infirmity, and the spirit of suicide. You cannot have our children, our families, or homes. You cannot have our businesses or churches. Your plans, devil, are cancelled and are consumed today by the Fire of the Holy Ghost.

Day 123
Morning Prayer (Part 4)

Thank you that our children have the wisdom to not listen to those who seek to do crime or mischief and seek to harm, not uplift. Help our children to make a quality decision to put your good ways before them, to remember the Word that was deposited in their hearts and minds. We call on that Word, which is indestructible, which will never fail, which endures throughout all times.

Day 124
Morning Prayer (Part 5)

We declare today that we shall live and not die to declare the mighty works of the Lord right here on Earth. We proclaim the promises here on Earth, the promises of victory, success, salvation, blessing, hope, love, and peace, in Jesus' name.

Day 125
Morning Prayer (Part 6)

We dedicate ourselves to a lifestyle that produces freedom in our lives and the lives of others. We are equipped to break the chains of injustice and untie weights of burden in Jesus' name.

We recognize and declare light has come. God, You have sent your Son, Jesus Christ, that we would not be destroyed, but so we might have life without end. That our life on Earth would be abundant. Let us learn today to cast our cares upon You because You care for us. Hear our prayer, God, and protect and promote your people for Your glory. Amen.

Day 126

I want to thank kids of pastors and community leaders. Please recognize that these special individuals had to learn how to share their parents.

Many times, when they wanted their parent's undivided attention, they had to share them with strangers. May God bless them all in a special way. I am talking about coaches, teachers, after-school attendants, and countless others who devote their time in making a difference.

Perhaps He will use you to be a conduit of blessing to them.

Day 127

I am talking to you.

We often gloss over details. We hear an instruction or teaching and think about someone other than ourselves, that this sermon would be great for our "friend or family member." Although, this attitude in many respects is laudable, please consider attending with an ear to hear what specific lesson is designed for you. I think if you practice this posture, you'll gain insight and creativity to address a myriad of situations and advance your personal development.

Think about it.

Day 128

On Mother's Day, we celebrate our heroes.

I love women, they are fearfully and wonderfully made. They are designed to help meet the perfect plan of God on the Earth. They are a gift to us and represent God's love. We would not be here without women, and Jesus Christ chose to be born of a woman.

I can be a man and appreciate the greatness in women. It is unfortunate that many voices make it seem like you must choose sides. This way of thinking is utterly ridiculous. I believe women add value to everything. They have a God-given ability to make things better. With that said, I think both men and women should endeavor to learn how to better relate to one another.

Please list two or three women in your life or in history whom you admire. What habits and/or qualities do they exemplify?

_____
_____
_____
_____

List two or three qualities you hope to represent in your life.

_____
_____
_____
_____

Day 129

Africa, Spain, Israel, Japan, China, Peru, Jamaica, Barbados, and Denver, Colorado: reaching the apex of Mount Elbert, California, Florida, and Atlanta, Georgia. I am already there and looking forward to travel.

Life is seasonal...winter, spring, summer, and fall.
This unusually troublesome season of COVID-19 has come and will pass. Amen.

I want to send my thoughts and prayers to those who have been negatively impacted by this wretched disease of COVID-19. Those who linger with effects of the disease, I speak healing and health to your body, mind, and spirit. To those who have lost loved ones, I offer my sincerest condolences to you and your family. I pray for your strength and peace. May God continue to keep you during this difficult time.

Day 130

As a parent, I have to remind myself that it is my responsibility to give my knowledge and wisdom to my children. It is their responsibility to listen to instruction. It can get frustrating at times, but I trust they will get it.

Day 131

When I look into the faces of my children, I know that I am loved. Thank you, Lord.

Sometimes children can make you gray a lot sooner than you normally would. Other times you feel like pulling your hair out or using an alias.

Do yourself a favor—take a step back and look at how remarkable they are.

Day 132

Wealth Matters - Read Psalm 112

Day 133

"Your Word is a lamp to my feet and a light to my path."
Psalm 119:105 (NKJV)

Don't fret, don't be overcome with fear, have faith to know that the Word will guide you along the way.

"Be strong in the Lord and in the Power of His might."
Ephesians 6:10 (NKJV)

PEACE.

Day 134

Use rejection and opposition to propel you further.

Let it be your fuel, like food, giving you the subsistence and determination to reach for your vision and goals. Don't let anyone or anything get in the way of your God-designed destiny.

Day 135
"Discipline is the bridge between thought and accomplishment."
– Dr. A.R. Bernard, Pastor of Christian Cultural Center

Day 136
"I know it may not be easy but I encourage you today to give it another try."
-Esjae, music artist/actor/fashion designer

Sometimes the struggles of life, make you want to throw in the towel and quit. Your promise and victory is worth fighting for. Don't give up.

Day 137
If you already know, you can avoid getting played.

We all appreciate admiration. "Hey, you look nice," etc. However, some males and females often use flattery to inflate the ego of their subject, only to get what they want and bounce. Don't get played. Know your worth.

I'm amazed how flippant and nonchalant we are with our most precious possessions. We live in a day where people don't reserve intimacy/sex for those who are worthy or special. We give it up at a click of a mouse. Really!

Ladies, then you want him to put a ring on your finger. Please!

Fellas, you want to be trusted and have someone devoted to you. How is that possible when you treat women with such disdain and disrespect? C'mon, bro!

Hey folks, I don't want to come off like someone who has been pristine all their life because that would be totally false. I deal with stuff just like everyone else. I went to college and exhibited behavior I'm not proud of. Truth be told, I made mistakes and lots of them, but I have a desire to do better. We got to do better, y'all.

Ladies, if you are looking for a king, start in the mirror. Examine who you are as a person and begin to develop into the best version of yourself by acknowledging God first and allowing his Word to instruct your life and behavior.

Similarly, fellas, if you are looking for your queen, you have to ask yourself why that ideal sister would render her value and virtue to you. You must be about something, doing something, going somewhere, able to provide and/or contribute to the basic needs in life, while providing physical and spiritual food and guidance to the family.

Please know God does not require you to have it all together. He works with our desires and beliefs. If you desire better and believe God can give you the wherewithal to succeed in life, then you are well on your way.

Note: Focus on your path, and don't get distracted by looking at others.

Day 138
Do You See Me?

A kid somewhere is asking that question. Our kids are unbelievably resilient, brilliant, and full of potential. They just need someone like you to notice their potential and spend a little extra time to tell them that they matter. Will you make the investment?

Many prominent people were literally saved by people who saw their humanity and decided to give of themselves. Without fanfare, these heroes went above and beyond. They are coaches, counselors, pastors, mentors, teachers, siblings, grandparents, cousins, aunts, and uncles. Everyday people doing extraordinary things.

I encourage you to be named among those who have decided that their life and blessings are not only for their enjoyment, but to be used to spark the brilliance in others.

Day 139

The earth provides answers—tilling the ground, planting seeds, watering, and then the harvest. All the elements are here for you to live...

We must decide each day, what to do with the raw material.

Day 140

"True friends are people that know your past, believe in your future, and are here for you now, and can be self-expressed in this journey of life!" – Alvin Clayton

What are the characteristics of a friend? Think about it and write down 1-5 attributes that you value in a friend.

1.

2.

3.

4.

5.

I have told my friends that they can be free to tell me good news and bad. I want to be the type of friend who can hear, empathizing with their struggles and shouting for joy with their triumphs. I want to be someone who is honest and authentic. I would rather tell a friend the truth in love, than to have them suffer the consequences because I did not want to hurt their feelings.

I believe true friendship is about being real with one another and learning to share of yourself. This sounds easier than it actually is.

Trust and communication is built over time and provide a link for deeper connection.

Day 141
Green new deal for public housing?

I grew up in public housing. People should not live in buildings that are unsafe and in disrepair. I think the focus should be on grants for residents to open businesses, to support entrepreneurship, provide education through scholarships, and encourage home ownership.

Day 142
"The only place success comes before work is in the dictionary."
– Vince Lombardi

Day 143
On principle. I'm going to like photos that don't show me everything. Dang.

Call me old fashioned, but I rather not see it all. The internet is laden with photos of people revealing nearly every part of their anatomy. I'm just not a fan of it. I realize some may find it liberating. I get it and understand it. But those same individuals must also understand that you attract a certain energy with how you present yourself. You want someone to appreciate your mind and personality, however, you only reveal your body. You say folks should be mature enough to see past your bikini/speedos, but that's easier said than done. The reality is those outfits are designed to accentuate your curves/physique, and they work.

Let your beauty emanate from the inside out. Think about the image (message) you are conveying with your dress and presentation.

Day 144
Okay. Let's help each other with some elder wisdom.

My grandfather, Taft Brewton, told me many things I still hold and use today. Below, please find results of a community exercise and survey I conducted online. I encouraged my friends to submit a favorite saying or quote from an elder who has helped them along the way. I hope these words of wisdom add to your life.

- "It's a full-time job minding your own business." *–Taft Brewton*

- "The early bird catches the worm." *– Submitted by Sheila Small*

- "Don't borrow from Peter to pay Paul." *– Submitted by Edith Rowe*

- "Everything that glitters ain't gold!" *– Submitted by Terri Small*

- "You don't need a bunch of friends." *– Submitted by Diedra Williams*

- "Don't burn the bridge, you may have to cross over again one day." *–Submitted by Lisa Woods*

- "All knowledge don't come from books baby." *– Submitted by Tempakius Tempest Watkins*

- "Don't buy what you want and then beg for what you need." *- Submitted by Tonya Iris Small*

- "Respect your elders." *– Submitted by Sharon James*

- "Don't watch people, watch how they treat you." *– Submitted by Denique Isme*

- "You can lead a horse to water, but you can't force him to drink." *– Submitted by Karen Stowe*

- "If you are right, go down fighting. If you are wrong, be quiet."

    – Submitted by Judith Henry
- "Learn from my scars." *–Submitted by Matthew McKines*

- "Once a man, twice a baby." *–Submitted by Taft Brewton*

Day 145

I'm good, brother. I'm good, sister. Just calling to say I love you.

I want to encourage you to consider those special people in your life. Spend the time to let them know you care for them. Let them know they matter to you. I know you're busy, but take the time today to call someone and let them know you care. You'll be surprised how much this gesture means to them.

Day 146

If I tried to sell you air, you would look at me like I was crazy. Yet, we often fall for it when someone or something beckons, "You need me or it in order to be special, unique, gifted, blessed, liked, successful, etc." Recognize that you were created astonishingly amazing!

Day 147

*Preciate it. Yup preciate it, sounds like preciated, short for **appreciate it**.*

Yesterday, I had an early morning workout. When I got home last night, my workout clothes were washed, dried, and folded. C'mon folks, all together now...preciate it. The journey to our next level in life is made easier when we have an attitude of gratitude. Practice appreciation daily.

What are you thankful for today?

_____
_____
_____

Day 148

Emotional Financial Proficiency (EFP) - The relation and importance of emotional and self-awareness as it relates to financial proficiency or the ability to adhere to financial principles.

-Omar Small

The concept of Emotional Financial Proficiency delves into why people make the financial decisions they do, the relationship between those decisions, and one's emotional and self-awareness. Greater self-awareness will help people understand their behavior as it relates to money management.

Did you witness a parent who saved and saved, but died young? Did people around you have a "you can't take it with you mentality," so there was very little concern about financial planning? Was there scarcity and fear as it relates to money, so money was not to be used for enjoyment or anything frivolous? Was money used as a status symbol and something attached to one's self-concept or self-worth?

It is my hope that through greater self-awareness, people will make better financial choices, allocating their resources for the benefit of themselves, their families, and their communities.

Day 149
Your words are like a prayer.

I received a call from a contractor today who has worked for me over the years. He was just checking in on me and the family, expressed his love, and said that he likes to hear me talk, that my words were like a prayer to him. Wow. You just never know the impact you make in other people's lives. They ascribe a positive feeling or express gratitude for an act of kindness you did. The cool thing is that you did it without thinking about it.

Has anyone ever recited something you said or reminded you of a good deed, and you totally forgot about it? If the answer is yes, keep doing what you're doing. If the answer is no, keep doing good and you're likely to have a similar experience.
Reference: Matthew 6:1-4

Day 150
You have to get in the water. You don't learn how to swim on the deck of the pool or on the seashore. You have to get your feet and body wet.

If you are learning a new skill or profession, you have to do what it takes to be proficient at it. If you desire a different lifestyle, you must expose yourself to a new setting.

Is there an aspiration or goal you want to achieve that is unfamiliar to you? A new career or business?

Have you begun to expose yourself to that new environment or familiarize yourself with the language and laws germane to this new area?

Day 151
You can be right or you can make progress. You get to choose.

Day 152
Early morning nuggets. Stay tuned.... It's a good one.

While reading the book of Genesis, I noticed something. I have read the account several times before, but I never understood this or paid close attention to the facts. The patriarchs of the faith, Abraham, Isaac, and Jacob, and their sons had many wives. Some of their wives were initially maidservants. One could easily surmise these maidservants were people from different tribes and ethnicities. What's amazing here is that God did not intervene as He did in the story of the Tower of Babel where He diffuses the language of the people trying to build a tower to reach the heavens.

To me, this fact helps to make clear that God promotes diversity. We may have different skin complexions, customs, and cultures but God created man or mankind in His image and likeness. He created one race, the human race.

One need only to look outside the window to see the diversity in creation—in flora and fauna, creatures on land and sea. If there is any question, God makes a statement that defines His love for mankind. It is found in John 3:16 (NKJV), *"God so loved the **World** that He gave His only son, that whoever believes on Him would not perish but have everlasting life."*

Whoever you are and whatever your station in life is, God loves you with an everlasting love. He has provided a way for every man, woman, and child on Earth to be a member of the family of God. My desire is that you are encouraged to seek Him and find the saving grace of Jesus Christ.

Another nugget or truth that proves God is into diversity: the way to God is made simple. Acknowledge God, confess your need for Him, accept His son, Jesus Christ, as your personal Lord and Savior, and you will become a member of the family. If that is not inclusionary, I don't know what is. Be encouraged today. Know that you are loved by God. He wants you to trust, love, and accept Him so you can be all He has designed you to be. I love you and pray this book has added value to your life.

Day 153
I am betting on the greater God placed in me.

Day 154
Shout out to all the Sunday school teachers and individuals who give back to our young people by speaking life over them. As a kid growing up in the housing projects, the deposit of the invincible, indestructible, incorruptible, and all-encompassing Word of God was invaluable.

Day 155
"I think one of the reasons we find it so easy to tear each other down is that we've often invested so little in building each other up."
— Shawn Rochester, Author, Educator, Business Leader

Day 156
When life squeezes you, what comes out?

Day 157
Keep moving forward. Let your past propel you onward and upward. Don't go back to the mess, but confess and confirm your ground, realizing you're not finish yet. You got a ways to go. Now let's go!

4:30 AM...Just getting started, I let my dog out and upon his return, a dog treat. Shortly thereafter, he began to convulse like he would vomit. I tried to rush him to the back door but before I was able to get him out, he began to throw up. I had him stay outside while I cleaned up. After cleaning, I took out the trash and let him back in.

He immediately went to an area I did not see before, an area where he began to throw up. At that moment, I was reminded of a caution described in Scripture found in Proverbs 26:11 (NKJV). *"As a dog returns to his own vomit, So a fool repeats his folly."* What a valuable instruction.

Refuse to go back to a behavior or habit, attitude, lifestyle, or relationship that does not sustain you. Don't go back to something that is formed for your defeat. No! Make a quality decision today to learn from your mistakes.

You should ask yourself why you're considering something that YOU KNOW does not benefit or add to your life. Is it an area of trust that needs to be fortified? Do you believe God has more for you? Do you believe God has better for you? If you are struggling with these questions, answer this: Does God love you?

YES, to infinity and beyond. His love for you is everlasting. In fact, He declares in Jeremiah 29:11 (NKJV), *"For I know the thoughts that I think toward you, says the Lord, thoughts of peace and not of evil, to give you a future and a hope."*

Spend a few moments thanking God for your life, health, and strength. Thank Him for the strength you exercised getting out of that bad situation. Thank Him that you can read and/or hear these words. Thank Him for the love you now feel in your heart.

Continue to move on and grow. Don't go back to your mess, let your past propel you forward. Let your past bring you to a place of gratitude, realizing God has more in store for your life.

Day 158

Consider this. Look at it and think about it. If your friends don't assist you to accomplish your goals, are they your friends?

Day 159

"The mind is a garden in which thought flowers grow, the thoughts that we think are the seeds that we sow."
– Author Unknown

Day 160

We were made in the image and likeness of God. We should pray and work toward being conformed to that image daily. Our collective pursuit would heal our world.

Day 161

"You look like you belong everywhere you need to be."
– Marshall Manigault

I had just dropped my truck off for a detailed cleaning in a neighboring town. I was familiar with the community, so I decided to walk around.

I went to the farmer's market, looked at upcoming development projects, and strolled through small parks. My plan was to find a bench and get some reading in, then head back to get my truck. As I walked down the avenue, a motorist honked his horn. It was Marshall, and I have known him and his family for decades. We grew up in the same housing complex, the Hollow, in New Rochelle, New York…345 and 361 Main Street.

I told him briefly what I was doing in town, and he quickly replied, "Hey brother, you look like you belong everywhere you need to be."

He said it. I felt it. I actually practice it. I practice and coach myself to feel comfortable wherever I happen to be.

References: Psalm 24:1 and Proverbs 29:25

Day 162
RULES

So interesting how folks change rules for their benefit or simply ignore the concept of rules. There are rules to everything. It's not a bad thing, it's just reality. I could talk about gravity and other rules, there are plenty of examples.

Let's talk about occupations. Would you want someone to build your house, who did not know the rules or concepts of construction? Would you want someone to operate on you who just felt like being a doctor that day? Would you want someone to drive you, not knowing the rules of the road? No. You have to ask yourself why people are trying so hard to dupe us into thinking that rules don't exist. That universal law is a figment of our imagination. PLEASE.

Day 163
PECULIAR

Some positive ways to view the term peculiar: atypical, different, out of the ordinary, rare, special, and particular. Each of us were made with uniqueness, being one of kind. Let God reveal to you how very special and unique (peculiar) He has called you to be.

Day 164
What was designed to separate us (coronavirus), will cause us to become stronger and more unified. Call someone today and encourage them. Tell them God will never leave them nor forsake them. Think about ways to be a light and refreshing to others. Send positive vibes...

Reference: Hebrews 13:5 (NKJV)

Day 165
Wisdom, you're my sister. A prayer for direction.

Wisdom, be close to me like a sister. When I need direction and clarity be present and available to me. Wisdom, protect me like a loved one. Let me know when I am heading down the wrong road and lead me back to the narrow path toward my destiny and purpose. Hint: Wisdom is found in the Bible.

Day 166
Spent the week in Charleston, South Carolina.

I gained so much insight. I talked to the people. I sat and observed. To my people in Charleston, I recite Philippians 1:6 (NKJV), "being confident of this very thing, that He who has begun a good work in you will complete it until the day of Jesus Christ."

I will never forget the Emanuel 9. On June 17, 2015 a wrongheaded idiot and hate-filled white supremacist/ domestic terrorist entered Charleston's Emanuel African Methodist Episcopal Church during a Bible study. This coward open fired, killing nine, whose names are listed below:

- Clementa C. Pinckney (41) – the church's pastor and a South Carolina state senator.

- Cynthia Marie Graham Hurd (54) – a Bible study member and manager for the Charleston County Public Library system; sister of former state senator, Malcolm Graham.

- Susie Jackson (87) – a Bible study and church choir member. She was the oldest victim of the shooting.

- Ethel Lee Lance (70) – the church's sexton.

- Depayne Middleton-Doctor (49) – a pastor who was also employed as a school administrator and admissions coordinator at Southern Wesleyan University.

- Tywanza Sanders (26) – a Bible study member; grandnephew of victim Susie Jackson. He was the youngest victim.

- Daniel L. Simmons (74) – a pastor who also served at Greater Zion AME Church in Awendaw, South Carolina.

- Sharonda Coleman-Singleton (45) – a pastor; also a speech therapist and track coach at Goose Creek High School; mother of former Major League Baseball prospect Chris Singleton.

- Myra Thompson (59) – a Bible study teacher.[14]

During my trip to Charleston, I wanted to visit the church and attend a Bible study to pay my respects to the Emanuel 9 and their families. There was a convocation the week of my visit, so the church was not open for regular services. Although, I was unable to go inside to attend a Bible study, I walked the church's perimeter and offered prayers. I had so many mixed emotions, walking that hallowed ground. One central thought was the devotion of the Emanuel 9 should never be forgotten.

So, as we persevere and push for justice, we should be reminded and empowered by those who have gone before us. We should recognize and appreciate those who have paid the price for us to enjoy a better day. Please remember the Emmanuel 9 and pray for their loved ones.

It is important for us to recognize those who have gone before us, whether they be family patriarchs or matriarchs, veterans, freedom fighters, and those seeking peace and justice. Please consider these heroes and let their desire for right live on. Think about it.

Day 167
"Just do your job. If everyone did their job, the world would be a better place."

– Edgerrin James, NFL Hall of Fame Running Back

Day 168
I'm their mother.

After the divorce, my mom raised all five of us on her own. She recounts a conversation she had with my grandfather, "You're going to have to be momma and papa." Whether this comment was a suggestion or quip in jest, my mom took offense. "No! I'm their mother." She was clear that by no means could she be both mother and father. She understood that her strength and calling was to be who God designed her to be, and that is a beautiful mother to her children.

How many people are duped into trying to be everything for everybody? It's just not realistic and is a cause for much anxiety, squander, and frustration. You can only be you. Think about it.

Day 169

"The truth is... justice will never come if we're unwilling to be uncomfortable. More people need to be willing to do the uncomfortable things that justice requires for anything to actually change."

- Bryan Stevenson

Day 170

Happy Father's Day: A salute to the fathers.

I want to wish all the men raising children and those providing a positive role model to children a Happy Father's Day. Research studies point to the negative impact of fatherlessness, which is defined as the state of having no father because he is dead or absent from the home. Social problems such as suicide, crime, teenage pregnancy, poverty, and poor school performance have been attributed, in part, to fatherlessness.

Unfortunately, some of the debate has focused on how impactful or important the role of father is in the home. I do not care to entertain that question, as it is common sense to understand that a caring and active father is of great significance to children, women, families, communities, and our society. I am interested in the impact that single women face when the fathers of their children are not present or supportive.

Compared to married mothers with jobs, single working mothers in the United States have a higher risk of heart disease and stroke, researchers found. They're also more likely to smoke—a known heart risk—than women with other work and family patterns, said Frank van Lenthe, co-author of the new study.[15] Losing the support of a partner, along with the second income, "may cause stress and result in unhealthy behaviors," said van Lenthe. He is an associate professor of social epidemiology at Erasmus University Medical Center in Rotterdam, Netherlands. Raising a family can be stressful, and those stresses can be multiplied when women or men do not have the support of the other parent.

To all the fathers holding it down and doing what is necessary for their children and families, I applaud and appreciate you. To men who have not been present for whatever reason, I want to encourage you to recognize the importance of your active presence. You should also know that the mother of your children needs your healthy respect and concern. Why? If your child's teacher was going through a rough divorce, dealing with emotional issues, or struggling with a substance abuse problem, those private issues could impact how he or she instructs and/or counsels your child. Now think about your child's home environment and their mother feeling overworked, abandoned, and stressed out. What kind of setting is being cultivated for the peace, growth, and development of your child?

I think I need to say something here. Often, when you describe an ideal, folks will feel the need to say, "I'm a product of a single mother household, and I turned out okay." That would be yours truly as well. I also think those same individuals would surmise that their childhood could have been bolstered and positively impacted by the presence of a caring and active father. For me, I was fortunate to have older brothers who shielded me from negative behaviors, strong male role models like my grandfather, Taft Brewton, and other men in the community who provided a positive outlet through sports, physical activity, and social engagement.

I'll share an adage that describes the power of a caring and active father. I hope you share it with the young people you love. A simple, yet profound statement, "I will hold the ladder, and you climb as high as you can." This statement gives the imagery of a son or daughter being encouraged to climb as far as they can with a supportive father at the end of the ladder, providing the encouragement for them to keep going.

Our children are brilliant. What would our world look like if we provided the stability and guidance they needed to reach their full potential? Calling all the fathers back to the children.

Day 172
She could be my daughter.

She looks nice, and perhaps she thinks I'm younger than I am. Two things…I'm spoken for, and she could be my daughter. I appreciate the reaction when I tell a young person my age. I've been out with my sons and got the older brother comment. I think that comment was just flattery, but it felt good, nonetheless. Now that I'm sporting a little salt and pepper, it's much easier to make the distinction.

Beyond the thought of, "Hey I still got it," I try to offer advice and consideration. She is young, impressionable, and perhaps there is something I can share with her that will help her move forward. Maybe the level of respect and honor given will be a good example of manhood. If she comes away from the encounter feeling respected, valued, and hopeful, then I've done my job. She could be my daughter.

Day 173
You work, I work, we work, and it's going to happen.

Day 174
You are so beautiful!

You must know and appreciate your worth whether or not you get likes on your social media posts. Our society is geared to have people focus on the external to validate the internal. I would encourage you to flip it, let the internal validate the external. Let your beauty come from the inside out.

Day 175
Yes, there is turmoil, strife, confusion, and chaos. Yet, there is peace, prosperity, wisdom, and wealth. One reality does not diminish the other for now. However, for the believer, our mission is to dispel the darkness with light (love). Be the light, knowing we win and overcome evil with good.

Good and light apply powerful means required for victory. Please don't think or picture good in a defeatist manner. Reject rolling over and accepting whatever idea someone throws at you. Instead, remember God handles business righteously. Trust!

Day 176

We have to do better, people.

I am sick and tired of seeing posts online of people fighting in the streets. You have people who are holding their cell phones recording and the crowd egging it on. We'd rather see a fight, than stop a fight. What does that say about the condition of our thinking?

As a man thinks in his heart (mind) so is he. **Reference:** Proverbs 23:7.

When you consider the condition of our neighborhoods, you have to also consider the condition of our thinking.

Yes, there has been and continues to be discrimination and racism. Yes, there has been and continues to be poverty, crime, drugs, and despair. But we are more than conquerors/overcomers through Him who loved us. With God all things are possible. I firmly believe we can do all things through Christ who strengthens us.

We can have strong and vibrant communities filled with strong and vibrant families and businesses. Top-rated and well-equipped schools for our children. Beautiful and pleasant parks for our collective enjoyment and pleasure. Healthy food options to sustain a well-balanced mindset and lifestyle. These things and more are all attainable and within our reach. It all starts with our thinking.

To all my friends, PLEASE, PLEASE, PLEASE consider your replies to this type of buffoonery. When you see these type of posts online don't like it, demean it. Denounce it. Don't co-sign gutter mentality. Don't encourage it, discourage it. Hear my heart, folks. We have to do better.

Day 177

The Detroit Pistons didn't make Michael Jordan weaker—they made him stronger, nearly invincible on the basketball court. Your opposition is designed to make you stronger. Think about it.

Day 178
We are foundational.

If you want to build a house or a building, you've got to have a firm foundation. Although you may not see the foundation of the finished project, without it, the building/house is compromised and prone to collapse. Continue to be solid, my brother. Think about it.

Day 179
I'd rather catch up than clean up, Pastor Ray Hadjstylianos, Living Word Christian Church

Sometimes I find myself in a bind of my own doing. This often happens to me when I don't pump the brakes and take the appropriate time to make sound decisions. I recently moved from New York to Texas. My idea was to secure a moving company, let them do the long-range road travel while I and my family fly to Texas.

I did a simple internet search and called around. I received a phone call from one of the companies who said they were in the moving industry for twenty years, they were a family-owned business, and many served in the armed forces. Thank you for your service. As the representative explained the move and provided an initial quote I began to perk up. It sounded like a great deal.

Everything changed once I provided a down payment. I was asked for an inventory of items, and the initial quote ballooned 130%. Okay, my thought was to change or remove some items on the moving list to comply with the initial quote. This is when their true colors began to surface. The representatives were unwilling to work with me or provide a way I could comply with the initial quote. This was a red flag and I began to do what I should have done in the beginning.

I started to do research on moving rates, and the typical square feet allotted for the size of apartment or house. What I found was that the initial square footage quoted by the representative was grossly inaccurate to the norm. I checked the Better Business Bureau, and the Department of Transportation only to find out that the company had many complaints and were not authorized to provide the service.

I ended up requesting a refund, which I have not yet received after months of delay. Don't worry, I'm not giving up until I get my refund. I decided after that experience to rent a truck and drive down myself. What a headache and waste of time. I don't blame the "moving company," I blame myself for rushing the process and not doing my homework.

Have you ever got into a predicament because you were in a rush?

_____

_____

_____

A safeguard I will implement to avoid this situation in the future is to sleep on it or give myself time to do research before making the decision. How about you? What strategies can you implement to avoid making rash decisions?

_____

_____

_____

Day 180
I don't have blinders on. I am encouraging myself, and I share to encourage others.

During these trying times, we must cling to the promises of God. If you are a believer, the current times should not dictate your beliefs, but reinforce what you believe. Read Jeremiah 29:11.

Day 181
We are designed to make things better.

I should make things better in my home, work, business, family, community, and church. Are others better because of you? Do things run better because of you? Acknowledge God with your life so you can fulfill your design. We need better.

Day 183

When do you let it go? Every day is packed with newness like no other day. There will never again be a day quite like today. My challenge is to understand and apply the value of yesterday, but don't allow the experience of yesterday to cloud today.

Day 184

If you want it, you want it. If you don't, you don't. Be honest and deliberate. Give yourself the best opportunity. Go for it.

Day 185
CHOICE

"I Want Somebody to Love Me for Me," a song by MC Heavy D— I was talking to a friend about relationships, and some have a thought of marriage as bondage. I think relationships should imitate God in that He gives us the choice to love Him.

I want my wife to decide each and every day to love yours truly. Who wants a relationship in which their significant-other feels trapped or unfulfilled?

Note: Sometimes the issue in these relationships is an unresolved past hurt, a relationship problem, or incompatibility. There may also be unrealistic expectations placed on a spouse, a void that can only be filled from a personal relationship with God.

I think the strongest relationships are built on trust and choice, a personal commitment to love in good times and in times of trouble. This sentiment was conveyed in a strong way by my Uncle Dennis who shared with me his love for my Aunt Brenda. They recently celebrated forty-eight years of marriage. He shared, "When she is not around, I feel like something is missing. My last breath, I'll be thinking about her. I want to be with her." Powerful and moving words of someone who decided to love through it all.

Although I have seen people grow apart, break up and divorce, I've also witnessed people who, through trust and choice, build a dynamic and vibrant love that grows in dimension and brilliance over time. Marriage is supposed to be two people trying to out-bless the other. I want that. How about you? I believe it's possible when two people commit to learn, love, and grow.

Day 186

Picture debt as a monster and you are the hero. The sword fits you. It chose you and came to you. Pursue that monster and off with its head! Crush debt and slay the dragon. Then live happily ever after.
Using your imagination, picture your victory. See yourself with both hands raised. Envision your debt destruction plan in place. Picture how you put in the work and kept your behaviors in line with your goals. See yourself investing more for your family and future. Don't lose momentum and keep going no matter the opposition. Refuse to go back to a life of servitude. Make money work for you.

Day 187

Expose someone to the truth today. John 3:16

Day 188

Be different. You were made to be unique.

Important tip: Let your difference give honor and glory to God.

Day 189

Doing for others and taking the focus off yourself is helpful in keeping a positive attitude.

Research shows that being kind and considerate to others can benefit your mental health and wellbeing by reducing stress, improving mood, and self-esteem. Helping others may also promote changes in the brain that are linked with happiness.[16]

These and a myriad of other benefits are associated with being generous and kind, including being able to give and a promise of prosperity. God supplies seed to the sower, and a generous person will prosper; whoever refreshes others will be refreshed. **References:** 2 Corinthians 9:10 and Proverbs 11:25

Day 190
Food for thought...what are you consuming these days? Healthy food?
Positive, wholesome thoughts? Inspiration?

List a book or an informational video/teaching that you have read or
viewed in the last ninety days. What does your list say about your
direction? Is your list in line with your goals?

_____
_____
_____

Day 191
"Whatever is worthwhile is worth working, striving, sacrificing, and
struggling for."
  – Ralph J. Bunche, Nobel Prize 1950, diplomat, Civil Rights advocate
and educator

Day 192
"You have to respect your time, otherwise others won't."
  – Kenneth Kweku Sr, Kweku Strategies

Day 193
"If you want to improve your life, you should choose your thoughts
every day, like you choose your clothes."
  – Elizabeth Gilbert

This is a simple instruction but can be difficult to put into practice.
When you want to think positive, negative thoughts flood your mind. I
try to replace the negative thoughts with a positive thought
immediately through prayer and/or positive affirmations. Below are
several examples.

- <u>You think about a person who did you wrong</u>.

Instead of allowing anger and frustration to overtake your thinking,
pray for that person. "Lord, whatever they are going through, please
help them." I have found this practice keeps me from focusing on the
individual and frees my mind and thoughts. It's not about the other
person, it's about you and your ability to move forward. Harboring

negative thoughts about another person does nothing but harm you and keeps you from progressing.

- You keep repeating something you didn't do well, beating yourself up.

Take your medicine. If there is something you omitted or intentionally did, acknowledge it, then affirm the positive. Speak out loud, *"I can do all things through Christ who strengthens me,"* Philippians 4:13 (NKJV). Another amazing promise from God: *"If we confess our sins, He is faithful and just to forgive us our sins and to cleanse us from all unrighteousness,"* 1 John 1:9 (NKJV).
Audibly, tell yourself, "I can do it, because I have greatness on the inside."

- You had a heated argument with your spouse, and the dispute is all you think about.

Pray about the situation, pray for your spouse, and resolve to discuss the manner when tempers cool. Apologize for where the discussion went. **Hint:** If it was a shouting match, the discussion went too far. Develop rules of engagement with boundaries on how you speak to your lover.

- You have unhealthy thoughts about someone who is in a committed relationship, a married man or married women.

Pray for the success of their marriage.

When you train your mind to respond to negative thoughts with positive thoughts, you starve negativity.

Day 194
Can we really live on Earth and be citizens of heaven at the same time?

When Jesus' disciples asked Him how to pray, part of His instruction was for them to pray, "Let your kingdom come and let your will be done on earth as it is in heaven."

Our desire and intent should be to see the beauty, majesty, peace, unity, love, and blessing displayed and manifested on Earth as it is in heaven. Obviously, we have a lot to pray for and a lot of work to do. But the aim is clear, we should endeavor to walk/live in a way that brings the attributes and atmosphere of heaven to Earth.

Imagine people treating others like they were formed in the image and likeness of God. Think about it.

Day 195
Prepared song by Jill Scott

Been lettin' some old ideas go
I'm making room for my life to grow
I just wanna be prepared, yeah
I just wanna be, I just wanna be prepared

This song is a beautiful reminder that in order for you to realize your hopes, and dreams you have to be deliberate and intentional in moving toward them. This activity very often includes moving away from distractions, cutting off negative influences, and focusing intently on your goals.

Process, next level, graduation, success, opportunity. All these terms are interlinked with preparation, the action or process of making ready or being made ready for use or consideration. It is my hope that you anticipate, expect, and appreciate the preparation process.
What are you getting prepared for? Please share what actions you will take to move toward your objectives.

_____

_____

_____

Day 196
Pray. Then do or not do. But first pray.

Day 197
This was just what I needed:

*"The discretion of a man makes him slow to anger,
And his glory is to overlook a transgression."* Proverbs 19:11 (NKJV)

I'm good now...

Day 198

I wish I could clone you. That was the comment made to me by one of my female friends and co-workers. I initially thought it a complement, then I thought it was an indictment. A wise man told me it's both. I must be intentional about being a big brother, a father figure, friend, and mentor. What about you?

Day 199

Be conscious and careful.

Although I have freedom, not everything is beneficial for me to partake in. What might seem harmless to someone else, might be a red flag and danger zone for you. That is why you should be careful about taking cues from others who do not have your personal experience or share your personal goals or beliefs.

For example, if you have had a problem with substance abuse or alcohol, you know your triggers and just being in a bar-like setting or indulging "a little," can push you over the edge to abuse. If you know that about yourself, it would be less than wise to take the advice of someone who does not understand your situation and has not had your struggle. Know your limits. Better yet, listen to your conscious to steer clear from situations that can jeopardize your peace, well-being, and spiritual walk.

People who get caught up in precarious and bad situations, don't often get there overnight. It is usually a combination of bad choices and ignoring the many warning signs. How did the affair happen for that married man or woman? Perhaps it started with lack of communication in the marriage, spending more time away, and not investing quality time with one another. Sharing precious time and conversations with someone other than your spouse erodes a marriage. The grass is not always greener on the other side. To imply that it is, suggests there is something better that's missing.

Recognize that the other person who is so lovely and calming is not a part of your day to day life. Your interaction with them is just a snippet of your total life. You are only dealing with pleasant activities such as nice and comforting chats, coffee/tea, lunch, dinner, fun events etc. These activities give an unrealistic perception to the person who is involved in a "committed relationship," full of chores, responsibilities, stresses, and delayed gratification.

Be smart and invest in your relationship, business, health, and family. Don't be fooled by "the grass is greener syndrome." Know that the lawn on the other side must also be mowed, and you don't know what kind of pesticides have been used or what type of insects/creatures are lurking. Think about it.

Day 200

"Nighttime download. In your anger do not sin": Do not let the sun go down while you are still angry, [27] and do not give the devil a foothold." Ephesians 4:26, 27 (NIV)

The thoughts we think before sleeping can help us have more restful sleep or can disrupt our sleep. A 2016 study[17] found that continuous thinking about negative events in the past or future, known as "perseverative cognition," is a link between stress and sleep quality,. Conversely, observational studies[18] in which participants self-reported found a positive link between optimism and sleep behavior.

Thinking positively can help aid sleep, while excessive negative thoughts can disrupt sleep. To function optimally, we all need sufficient rest. Sleep is restorative for the body, repairing cells, muscles, organs, and the immune system. Better sleep is not only good for the body but can benefit your overall well-being and mental health.

Our health and wellness regimen should include getting sufficient rest. Substitute negative thoughts with prayer and positive affirmations. Cognitive reconstructing is a term used to describe a counseling technique of replacing negative thoughts with positive, more constructive thoughts. I have included two Scriptures below that describe the importance of positive thinking.

- Philippians 4:6-8 (NKJV)–*"Be anxious for nothing, but in everything by prayer and supplication, with thanksgiving, let your requests be made known to God; ⁷ and the peace of God, which surpasses all understanding, will guard your hearts and minds through Christ Jesus. ⁸ Finally, brethren, whatever things are true, whatever things are noble, whatever things are just, whatever things are pure, whatever things are lovely, whatever things are of good report, if there is any virtue and if there is anything praiseworthy—meditate on these things."*

- Romans 12:2 (NKJV) – *"And do not be conformed to this world, but be transformed by the renewing of your mind, that you may prove what is that good and acceptable and perfect will of God."*

Use the Scriptures, pray, and read good books. Listen to and/or recite positive affirmations replacing negative thoughts with positive thoughts. Don't let the stresses of the day rob you of your peace and opportunity to recharge. Be aware of your nighttime download.

Day 201

"This Week," a song by Anthony Brown & group therAPy, signified a shift and encouragement for my wife and me to trust God through a trying time.

We put our house up for sale on August 3, 2020. After some starts and stops, we finally got offers, with each one at asking price or a little higher. We went with the first offer, signed contracts, and anticipated the closing.

We planned to move south, and selling our home was the first step. It also indicated the time for me to inform my current employer that I would resign my position. Prior to the contract signing, I sought counsel from my pastor. I wanted to announce the changes immediately. He advised me to not make a move until the contract was signed, "Let the contract be the linchpin to your next move." This was excellent advice, and I am glad I listened.

My wife, realtor, and I encouraged each other by repeating our mantra, "This Week." This saying affirmed that our desired outcome would materialize soon. At work, my announcement to resign caught everyone by surprise, but I wanted to give sufficient notice to my employer. Shortly thereafter, my wife and I took a trip to find our next home. During a weekend, we saw over twenty homes. Our realtor in Texas went above and beyond.

We put in offers, but none were accepted. In addition, our criteria had changed. Although we initially agreed that a forty-five-minute ride from family members was okay, we quickly began to reconsider that notion and finally determined we wanted to live closer to family. We put an offer on a home. It was countered, and after discussion, we withdrew our offer. We did not find our next home on the trip, but we got a chance to see some nice homes and areas.

Back in New York, we continued to look at properties online and communicate with our realtor in Texas. He would go to open houses for us and provide access virtually. Knowing we had to find a suitable home, we put an offer on a property with the contingency that we had to sell our property in New York. We had executed contracts on our home. Our house in New York passed inspection and appraised approximately 2.5 percent higher than the asking price. We thought we were in a good position, as we had a contract on our home and executed a contract to buy a new home in the South.

After a year of planning, things seemed to be moving in the right direction. Then a sudden and grinding halt. The buyers requested contract extensions and ultimately did not obtain financing. Disappointing, but we had the right formula. We put the house back on the market, and again got multiple offers and accepted one that provided the most profit.

Again, things were moving toward the sale of our home and us finally moving. This time, the stall occurred due to issues raised by the buyer's counsel. I seriously questioned the last-minute objections. The buyers were clear to close, yet withheld that information for nearly a month. I felt the handwriting was on the wall, and this second deal seemed headed down the same path as the first.

Frustrated! I was upset over the process and began to question what God was trying to show me.

We planned and prayed, prayed and planned. I requested and received Godly counsel. We continued and increased our giving. We prepared the property for showings and readily accommodated requests to see the property. We were doing our part…what was going on?

Our plan was to sale the home, for me to resign from my job, and for us to be in our next place, while still receiving residual income and working my new business. Now with two deals gone sour, seven plus months passing, and residual income running out, my focus was more on selling our home than growing the business. I also had to relinquish a rental property. Without a steady source of income, it was difficult covering the mortgage and an apartment rental.

While the second deal dissolved, I made up my mind to sell our home myself. It was not a slight on my realtor in any way. She came highly recommended as a dynamic, responsible, and professional realtor. I just felt like I needed to control the process a bit more. My realtor was gracious enough to provide helpful tips, as well as faithful to repeat our mantra of, "This Week." She checked on us periodically, and soon I was able to sell our home to a lovely family. Smiles all around. ☺

During this process, I had to push through setback after setback. I had to remain steady although things were seemingly unraveling. I pushed through doubt and anxiety by keeping the faith. I continued to pray and believe in God's perfect timing. He revealed a better plan at the right time.

I sold our house for more money, and I was able to support family members during some stressful times. My business increased, and I made some great connections. In addition, I obtained a better roadmap for our next level.

Wow! I did not know how it would all turn out, but I was confident God would make a way for me and my family. I won't forget this process that took nearly fifteen months. I was definitely pushed outside of my comfort zone. At times it was disappointing and frustrating, but it all worked out for my benefit in the end. It happened "this week," but it took many weeks.

What do you do when things don't go according to plan?

    A. Scrap the plan and start over.

    B. Stay the course. It's just a matter of time.

    C. Assess whether the plan needs to be tweaked.

    D. Begin to doubt your ability to accomplish the plan.

    E. None of the above.

Have you had a circumstance in your life that did not go according to plan, but worked out better in the end?

Day 202

We've added so much. We've made it more difficult for people to accept and follow God. We've made it about ourselves rather than others. God, the Father, has provided all you need for salvation, and it starts with a choice that you believe in your heart (mind) and confess with your mouth.

I wrestled with thinking I had to do something or be something before I could make that choice. This thinking was faulty. As a parent, big brother, big sister, or friend, "Do you put restrictions on your loved ones before they can receive your love?" Most likely the answer is no. God does not, either. Just come to Him as you are. He knows you and knows exactly what you need.

A couple of thoughts: God does not design copies. You are unique, made wonderfully. Allow God the opportunity to show you how beautiful, brilliant, and remarkable you are. Trust Him today. I used to think that living for God meant I was going to be locked up, that it meant I could not do this or that, but it's quite the contrary. Now I realize I have tremendous freedom and I choose a lifestyle that is beneficial to me, my family, my community, and world.

References: John 3:16, Psalm 139:14, Romans 10:9, and John 8:32

Day 203

If it had not been for the Lord who was on my side,
_____ *(fill in the blank).*

Only you know where you were mentally, spiritually, and physically when God rescued you, gave you a new perspective, healed your body, gave you strength to carry on, or saved a loved one.

Please consider and chew on this statement. Know that it is a part of your victory, your journey, your testimony. This statement has the power to keep you grounded and humble, elevating you in every area of life. When you look back and really consider where you could have ended up, it will make you want to shout.

Raising your voice is one form of expression. There are so many more. Sometimes it's a song, a dance, tears of gratitude, silence, and overwhelming joy. Stay there, bask in it, and know, as you continue to walk, there is more to come.

Day 204

"There is value in your truth. Being honest with yourself is a building block and foundation for growth."
– Contribution by Sheryl Hatwood, Playwright, Director and Producer

Day 205

To become a champ, you often spar with champions.

Many great athletes, performers, and professionals developed their skills while playing against, performing, and working with more accomplished talent. Putting yourself out there with exceptional, gifted people may be daunting and nerve-racking, but it helps you to learn for yourself, and can be a catalyst to boost your drive and confidence.

I remember hearing advice for new graduates to either try to work for a great organization or a great or influential individual. The intent is to choose environments that will help you grow and tap your potential. Another technique is to study successful people and organizations to gain valuable insight.

Please list three goals that you would like to achieve in the next twelve to twenty-four months.

1.

2.

3.

Can you identify an organization, group, or individual that can assist and/or encourage you to achieve your goals?

_____

_____

_____

Pray about it. Lord help me to acknowledge and recognize the group, organization, or individual that can help me reach my goals.

Day 206
Thinking is so underrated. The quality of your life is immensely impacted by the quality of your thoughts. Pay attention to your thoughts. If you want to change your life, change your thoughts.

Day 207
You would be great.

Hearing those words might be flattering. When you bring your skills, aptitude, positive attitude, and essence to your daily activities, you're likely to hear people attempt to woo you with those words. It sounds great, right? Who could blame them for wanting you on the team? You are an exceptional person, and they are doing what any other smart businessperson would do—trying to get good people to work with them.

The question for you is whether the offer is your opportunity, a distraction, or something for you to ponder further. A distraction might be something that takes you away from your goals and objectives. Your passion is working with young people, and the offer is in a field you have no interest in.

An offer you may consider is one aligned with your goals and objectives. Is it the right setting or the right time? As a municipal administrator, I recall talking to people about opportunities to work for different cities, towns, and villages. These conversations were confidence builders, but each "offer" was not a firm one, nor the right one. As a family man, I had to weigh each potential opportunity with the stability and health of my family. How are the schools? Will I be able to afford relocating? Is the area safe?

Whether an offer is a distraction or an opportunity, you can benefit from analyzing the feedback and your response. When you know it's a distraction, do you immediately dismiss it, or do you entertain it because you are enamored with the gesture? If the offer lines up with your goals, do you take it immediately or determine whether it is the right deal for you? It is important to gather clues with each offer. What does the offer tell you about yourself, what you are good at, and what is your calling?

So, the next time you hear, "You'd be great," recognize that the statement may be true. Determine whether the offer is a distraction or opportunity, and use the information to gain insight on your talents, abilities, passion, and priorities.

Day 208

Yes. Yes. Yes. I can learn from you, you, and you.

"Out in the open wisdom calls aloud, she raises her voice in the public square." Proverbs 1:20 (NIV)

You are now in your twenties, thirties, forties, fifties, sixties, seventies, eighties or nineties. Even if you reach the tender age of 120, your life is yet a breath, a moment in time.

That is why we are to take advantage of every day, love on people, and give God glory by becoming the best versions of ourselves. Through each phase and stage of life there is much learning. A baby learns how to talk and walk. An elder on the other end of the spectrum may also need to learn those skills once more.

We have our degrees and symbols of distinction and status. We have had many different experiences in life. Like driving a car, we sometimes get to our destiny without taking in the details of the route. I would think there are pros and cons to living on automatic. Sometimes a rote response is necessary, and other times you might miss important information.

Take the time to assess where you are in life by acknowledging God. *"Trust in the Lord with all your heart (mind) and lean not on your own understanding. In all your ways acknowledge Him and He will direct your paths."* Proverbs 3:5 (NKJV)

Stay open to the process of learning. Hear the call of wisdom.

Day 209

"Stop dimming your light for those that can't handle your shine."
   – Kym Hampton, Women's National Basketball Association legend
                              Musician, actress, model, and spokesperson

When I sat down for an interview with Kym she explained her mantra, "Stop dimming your light for those that can't handle your shine." She said people who are really good at something sometimes scale it back or don't fully display their prowess to accommodate others, as an attempt to fit in. Others, who may feel inadequate due to their physical appearance, may also scale it back for the same reason. The need to fit in or be accepted is so strong, people downplay their gifts, talents, and abilities.

I think understanding the difference between humility and pride can unburden people and help them to unlock their full potential. Some folks think humility is a bad word, but I think humility is a beautiful and strong word. In this instance, humility dictates that an individual is true to his or her gifting and abilities. Humility is the opposite of being prideful, which is defined as an excessively high opinion of oneself. I think folks should avoid becoming prideful because it clouds their vision and mental acuity.

If you were a piano prodigy and your parents, teachers, or friends asked you to play a musical selection, it would be prideful for you to play "Chopsticks" in a condescending manner. It would be humble for you to vigorously play music from great composers like Scott Joplin or Margaret Bonds.

Another contrast between pride and humility: an athlete, boxer, team, or organization does not consider their opponent or competitor (prideful). They assume, because of their status and ranking, that their opponent or competitor has no chance. The team has an undefeated record, and their opponent does not have the same caliber of athletes. In the case of an organization, it has owned a particular market segment for decades. Their leadership team has an attitude of indifference toward other organizations and competitors just entering the marketplace.

You may have heard of athletes who lost a big fight or big game in large part because they did not train especially hard. Instead, they partied and did whatever they wanted, thinking their opponent was not worthy of any extra effort. Or, consider an organization that lost market share because they did not pay attention to the changing business climate and adjust accordingly like their "competitors." Both are examples of pride and resting on your laurels. The athlete, team, or organization could not perceive nor see the threat posed because of hubris.

Avoid pride by staying humble—that is working hard, trusting the process, doing all you can to prepare yourself, your team, or your organization for the next level and opportunity.

Can you identify with holding back a skill, talent, or aptitude because you wanted to fit in?

Shift your thinking. Displaying your talent, acumen, or capacity is being humble and generous. As you share your gift(s) for the betterment of others, people recognize your light (shine), and give God glory. See Matthew 5:13-16.

Please consider expanding your network to a group of people who can appreciate your gifts and help you to develop them.

Day 210
Alive and well. I want to extend a heartfelt good morning to everyone. Stay focused, stay prayed up, stay alert, and stay prepared. All the best moving forward.

Day 211
Speak Life.

With all this negativity swirling around, you might catch yourself saying the wrong things. You can acknowledge facts, but you must know and speak the truth. By speaking life, we come out of this thing stronger and more determined to succeed. We win!

Day 212
Don't Give Up. God is wit you. Sophia Small.

At first glance you would think I made a typo spelling with (wit). No typo—that's the way my five-year-old daughter wrote it. One day she found an old shoe box, put tape around, and made an opening at the top. She then took index cards and put positive messages on them and placed them in the box. She shook the box and invited us to pick one. Wow! What a heartfelt gesture to desire to create a device for the benefit and encouragement of others. Don't give up. God is wit you.

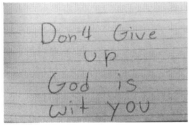

By Sophia Zoe Small

Day 213
Leadership is best in service.

Day 214

We are fascinated with things that flash, sparkle, or sizzle. We lionize people who do outrageous acts or those who flaunt their "status." We're enamored with the outer appearance and often don't take the time to see what's underneath the persona.

Some of these images are unhealthy and do not provide a good model for young people. Nevertheless, whatever sells, whatever gets me my fifteen minutes of fame, whatever it takes to be noticed, is what people subscribe to.

The need for acceptance and affirmation is a human need. In a todayonline.com article, Joanna Koh-Hoe, CEO, Focus on the Family-Singapore,[19] said her parenting workshop teaches parents that children have five main emotional needs: acceptance, affirmation, attention, affection, and accountability. I think that is true for children and adults. Today, in our digital world, we have had to use technology more and more. That is why social media platforms are so appealing. The heightened use of technology has magnified our need to connect emotionally.

In this environment, the person not on social media or someone who does not have a gazillion followers, may feel less than adequate. There are countless benefits to technology, however, overuse of it can have negative impacts. In a 2017 study[20] published in the *American Journal of Preventive Medicine,* higher use of technology was associated with a greater sense of isolation among young adults. Isolation can lead to feelings of depression and anxiety.

On October 5, 2021, former Facebook employee Frances Haugen testified before Congress that the choices being made inside of Facebook are disastrous for our children, public safety, our privacy, and our democracy. Haugen told Congress that Facebook consistently chose to maximize its growth rather than implement safeguards on its platforms, just as it hid from the public and government officials' internal research that illuminated the harms of Facebook products. [21]

Whether you believe these assertions of negative social impacts or not, use social media frequently or sparingly, it is essential for us to peel away from time to time and connect with those close to us in a real way. Instead of texting all the time, pick up the phone, write a letter, or meet your friends and neighbors in person. We must be deliberate to build community and strengthen the ties that bring us together.

How are you doing in this area? Do you need to peel away from social media? If you do, try to go without visiting social platforms or using your devise for short increments of time, several hours, a day, or more. It is all about your mental and physical well-being. Sometimes putting those gadgets down is just what the doctor ordered.

Day 215

A message sent to my nephews: Think about it. Write it down, pray about it, and begin to move toward it. Recognize the small victories. Learn from your setbacks, Dust yourself off, and continue to press, young man, press.

An awesome privilege I have is the ability and the opportunity to speak into the lives of my siblings' children, nieces and nephews. At times you can feel like they're not listening, but they are. They're listening and watching. Continue to sow into the lives of your loved ones with the life that you have been given. Pass it on!

Day 216

You must see, smell, taste, and feel your next level of development. Use all your senses to prepare yourself for it.

This picture is of a book I had in my mind. I knew one day I would complete it. Prior to completing the work, and getting the first printed copy, I pictured the book. I cut a paper bag and taped it to my journal with the title and author photo.

This is a picture of me signing a copy of my book yet to be produced and published. I repeat, use all your senses to prepare for your next level.

Day 217
My daughter made a peanut butter and jelly sandwich and allowed me to take it for breakfast. In fact, she put it neatly in a sandwich bag with a smile. Best breakfast I've had in a long time.

Day 218

Rest in peace, Sis. Just learned of the death of fashion trailblazer Mama Cax at thirty years old. Her life and victory will continue to inspire others. Respect.

When you look inside yourself and recognize your beauty and the brilliance of being created in the image and likeness of God, you'll appreciate your radiance and share your shine. I believe Mama Cax lived this statement in a very real and powerful way.

She was born Cacsmy Brutus on November 20, 1989 to Marie Vilus and Cacsman Brutus in Brooklyn, New York. The Haitian-American model was a beacon of hope to many as she revealed her struggles and triumphs to help unlock potential in others. During her teenage years she battled bone and lung cancer. Her right leg was amputated after an unsuccessful hip replacement.

Losing a limb was traumatic, and the adjustment was painful and difficult. For many years she did not see herself as beautiful and loathed her appearance. As she traveled and studied, she noticed that people with disabilities and scars were not well-represented. As a result, she began to write about her experiences to share with women in similar situations. Her transparency proved to be cathartic.

Her personal health challenges did not detour her from obtaining two post-secondary degrees in international studies. She continued to grow and share, while developing her voice and confidence. That voice, beauty, and essence would be revealed in 2017 when she landed her first advertising campaign. Soon thereafter, Mama Cax modeled for luxury fashion brands. She graced the cover of *Teen Vogue*, and was seen on runways at the White House and New York Fashion Week.

She was an advocate and shining example of perseverance, elegance, and beauty. Her life speaks volumes to all people, especially those dealing with physical disabilities, social barriers, and feelings of low self-worth. Actress, singer, fashion designer, and business woman, Rihanna, called Mama Cax, "A queen. A force. A powerhouse beauty."[22] May her life and legacy live on and inspire others.

Day 219

A friend told me I was one of his personal Sherpa. Humbling compliment to be considered a guide or someone who can provide guidance. It is our responsibility to be our brothers/sister's keeper.

I rely on this same friend to help me with topics related to the use of technology and other pertinent matters. Our relationship is an exchange. We enjoy talking about sports, family, politics, current affairs, and relationships, among other topics. I find that our ability to sharpen or enhance one another is of mutual benefit, which strengthens our friendship. He provides value, and I provide value. It is not one-sided in any aspect.

On the other hand, some relationships are marked by a lopsided dynamic. One person acts in a very selfish manner and seldom considers the other person. I am not talking about resources (money)…I am talking about intent and attitude. I have relationships in which people can give of their resources (money) in a greater way than I can currently give and vice versa. The key in those relationships is that I am willing to give of what I have. It may be a kind word, a listening ear, honest feedback, physical workouts, help during special events, manning the grill, providing childcare, or helping with a move.

It is important to consider your friendships and relationships as they are a great indicator of the direction and trajectory of your life. Although money is needed and is very important, a person's attitude, mentality, and thought process is much more important. Many people have made the mistake of judging a person based on how much money they think he or she has. Growing up, I could recall noticing an air of superiority in others, a raised eyebrow amongst some who, I believe, made judgements when they learned of my residence and neighborhood. I am sure they'd all agree now that considering the thinking and thought process of an individual, no matter what their station in life, is much more important. But I digress.

"All the brothers of the poor hate him; How much more do his friends go far from him! He may pursue them with words, yet they abandon him!" Proverbs 19:7 (NKJV). I believe this verse has little to do about money, and more to do with attitude and the willingness of the

"poor" person giving of himself. This individual is described "poor" because he does not seek to give anything. Not a hello, not a smile, not a handshake or a helping hand, not an open door, nothing. He is consumed with a poverty mentality or poor thinking. That does not lend to considering the plight or emotions of others, and is totally self-absorbed. No wonder his brothers despise him and his friends run from him.

Are your friendships mutually beneficial?

Does the mentality and thinking of your friends match what you want to achieve in life?

Have they helped or supported your vision? For example, you are a single mom trying to obtain your college degree. A friend might offer childcare services at no or reduced cost once or twice a week, so you can focus on your studies.

Day 220
Prepare for the long game.

Former heavyweight champion boxer Muhammad Ali, through superb ring generalship, allowed the younger/stronger George Foreman to exhaust himself in the "Rumble in the Jungle." When the champ tapped out, Ali unleashed a flurry of blows that knocked him out. Don't lose sight of your destination, don't get distracted. Instead, stay focused on the long game.

Day 221
Just because you can, doesn't mean you should.

Day 222
I'm ready for the wealthy place. God has deposited so much in me. It is time to share. This is a purpose question. What has God placed in you that is special and unique?

Do you have a way of making people smile or laugh? Are you compassionate and considerate? Do you have a special skill or vocation? Have you been through a rough patch in your life and come out on the other side? Do you have a desire to make a positive change? If so, God can help you discover how awesome you are. As you begin to realize your brilliance, help someone else unlock their brilliance. More life, more shine!

Day 223

Not easy, but necessary. Allow your kid to trip and fall. Oftentimes it is required, so that they gain strength, fortitude, and balance.

Day 224

Great day, people! God is faithful. The sun is out, birds are chirping, and the colors of fall are all about. Great day. Great opportunity. God is faithful.

Day 225

When you say yes to something, you are saying no to something else.

Day 226

On the road again. Just want to stay in my lane. What is your lane or focus?

_____

_____

_____

Sometimes we are not as effective or productive in our lives because we are so distracted and diffused. It's okay to cut some things off, so you can grow. Think about it.

Day 227

"This is my motivation right here. This is my drive each and every day, they are counting on me to win."
– Dylan Raymond, Military Transition Expert

Who is counting on you to win?

_____

_____

Day 228

Wisdom is the way out. Ask for wisdom. James 1:2-8.

Day 229

Keep saying yes to the greatness inside of you.

Day 230

Management is life. We are given time to manage our lives.

Day 231

The grass is greener right here. Sow, nurture, and reap your harvest in your field.

Day 232

Please think before you post. Some of the things said and done online are tragic and unfortunate. Do folks consider their parents, siblings, kids, or grandkids when they hit send? Apparently not.

Day 233

"In Pursuit of Justice" with Judge Jared Rice. Brother Smalls speaks with Judge Jared Rice about the social climate in the US, the court system, and criminal justice reform, http://brothersmalls.com.

Day 234

Word is life, so obtain good Word.

Day 235

We are all in need of the truth.

"Jesus said, 'You shall know the Truth, and the Truth shall set you free'" John 8:32 (NKJV). Until we can look in the mirror and say, "I need truth to better understand life, recognize and appreciate my fellow man, and gain personal insight," we will limit our development.

Day 236

PLM – Promise Land Mentality. Keep a Promise Land Mentality and focus on what the Lord has promised you.

Day 237

"The momentum is in the doing."
–Mark McLean, Generations Church/New Rochelle NAACP Local Branch President

Day 238

I woke up the other morning and said to myself, the birds will not out praise me. When you rise early, you know birds are getting it in, singing and chirping their praises. Well, I, for one, will not be outdone by birds giving praise to God. Think about it.

Day 239

I appreciate ministers and people of influence who speak the truth. I am concerned we don't hear from others who have the same charge and responsibility about the blatant disregard for human life. In fact, I don't know how you can call on the name of our Lord and Savior Jesus Christ and not be utterly disturbed by injustice.

Day 240

The fascinating and scary Shoebill bird. Look it up, but don't look directly into its face, "chilling." These impressive birds can position themselves and stand motionless for hours waiting to strike. What appears to be inactivity is not. Are you getting in position?

Day 241

Use your memory to combat complacency. Think back on where God has brought you from. Now is not the time to hold back, but to push forward into your land of promise.

Day 242

Truth over feelings. Sometimes we allow our emotions to cloud our perceptions. Feelings and emotions are important, and we should examine why we feel the way we do. However, we should not put our feelings over our God-given design and purpose. Stay focused, press through.

Day 243

Think of money as a power or a power source. What are you doing with your power? You can use your power to enrich others or use your money to empower yourself, your loved ones, and your community. With every exchange, I'm beginning to ask myself, "How did I use my power?"

Day 244

There is a defect in the design. Imagine going to a car dealership and explaining to the sales manager that the new shiny car in the display window is defective. I would think you would get a coarse response or at the very minimum a response touting the improvements, gas mileage, technology, and amenities in the vehicle.

I think it safe to say that these encounters are not the norm. Interestingly, we often view ourselves as defective or flawed. I don't mean flawed in a humble way that recognizes the need for improvement but flawed in a self-loathing way. We consider ourselves too tall, too short, too heavy, and too thin. We are not the right complexion, or we don't have the right letters behind our name. We are too young or too old. Folks this is tiresome. Are any of us perfect? No.

But we are all beautifully unique and special. Think about it.

Day 245

I am passionate about wisdom. I am passionate about Jesus. I am passionate about love. I am passionate about Jesus. I am passionate about life. I am passionate about Jesus. I am passionate about good. I am passionate about Jesus. I am passionate about knowledge. I am passionate about Jesus. I am passionate about wisdom...

Day 246

People of good conscious and humanity must stand for righteousness and truth, real reform, and not lip service. Those who want to empower and encourage the people for the betterment of society, must stand in solidarity against those of evil will and intent. We shall overcome.

Day 247

You are doing fine. Sometimes all we need is a word of affirmation. We are not finished yet, and we are all works in progress. Keep going...You're doing fine.

I consider myself a pretty good athlete and participated on many sports teams growing up. I appreciated coaches who would tell me how to better my game using encouragement instead of yelling or criticizing in a demeaning way. This type of reprimand would cause me to tune out anything that was being conveyed. It became a matter of respect for me. Give me the courtesy to explain what you are trying to accomplish. As I matured, I learned how to sift through boisterous and even communication I thought rude to obtain valuable information. I began to ask myself, "What is he/she trying to say?" I must admit, I sometimes get distracted with how a message is delivered and would prefer verbal discourse that is measured and calm, but that's just me. How about you?

Communication is about understanding and being understood. We sometimes have problems in this area because we don't recognize our personal style of communication nor consider the communication style of others. How many times have you shared a message that was not followed or misinterpreted? Sometimes it's them and sometimes it's us. Lyn Christian of SoulSalt Inc. said, "Powerful communication means understanding your needs and learning how to express them clearly — while also valuing the messages you receive from others."[23]

Social science has defined four basic types of communication.[24]

Passive Communication
- Not expressing feelings or needs; ignoring your own personal rights and allowing others to do so

- Deferring to others for decision making in order to avoid tension or conflict

- Often leads to misunderstanding, built-up anger, or resentment

- Can be a safer communication option when a conflict may escalate to violence

Aggressive Communication
- Expressing feelings, needs, and ideas at the expense of others; ignoring others' rights in order to support your own

- Defensive or hostile when confronted by others

- Often alienates and hurts others

- Can help meet your needs quickly

Passive-Aggressive Communication
- Appearing passive on the surface, but subtly acting out anger

- Exerting control over others by using sarcasm and indirect communication, or avoiding the conversation

- Limited consideration for the rights, needs, or feelings of others

Assertive Communication
- Direct, honest communication of thoughts and feelings

- Respecting the feelings, ideas, and needs of others while also asserting your own

- May not be effective when interacting with individuals that threaten your personal safety

- People often misinterpret assertive behavior as aggressive – Americans and women are often mislabeled as a result

This list is provided to help you discover your personal style of communication and understand the style of others. Please note these definitions are tools and are not absolutes. Our use of communication styles is fluid and vary based upon our social setting, and our mental and emotional states. I encourage you to continue to dialogue and be open to understanding your own voice and the voice of others.

Day 248

Timing is everything. Lord, you know who I am, please help me to take advantage of time. I need You to restore the years I have wasted and help me by Your Holy Spirit to stay on track.

Day 249

Use it or lose it.

Procrastination is a robber and thief. We often put off things for tomorrow that can be done today. Before you know it, days turn into weeks, weeks into months, and months into years. This phenomenon happens every day to people from all walks of life.
For some, they are fortunate enough to catch themselves and regain their direction and focus. For others, a window of opportunity is closed shut. I, for one, believe if you can inhale and exhale, there is opportunity. With that said, there are real timelines that cannot be ignored.

Consider a gymnast, athlete, police officer, or fire fighter to name a few professions that have age requirements and markers that cannot be avoided. If you miss a deadline, then you have lost an opportunity. Other occupations and endeavors may be pursued at various times, but it is not wise to wait to the last minute.

Activate, use, and hone your skills today. If you are a writer, keep writing. If you are a singer, keep singing. If you are a performer, find ways to share your gift. I recall having a conversation with a neighbor. He and I often share our thoughts and discuss matters of the day. One night I explained to him that I wanted to share my insight to a larger audience. What he said to me was affirming and sobering at the same time. "Yes, you got to use it, or it will become stale." This remark motivated me. I don't want to become stale, musty, dry, and old because of inactivity.

Time waits for no one. Think of a young person in your life who recently graduated high school, college, or is getting married/having a baby. We ask, "Where did the time go?" Did someone hit the fast forward button? No. Time is what we make it. Regardless of what we do with it, time will elapse. The question is whether you will use your time wisely or squander time and opportunity.

Now is the time to move toward your dreams. Now is the time to plan. Now is the time to live your best life. Now is your opportunity to make your mark. Don't let it slip away. As noted by author William Garcia, "It's now o'clock."[25] Use it or lose it.

Reference: Psalm 90:12

Day 250
I got life. You got life. Let's go!

Day 251
Barbershop talk about fatherhood.
As a father, I cannot think about not being in the lives of my kids. I don't get it. It's unnatural.

My barber: If you're not present, it is like you're running away from yourself.

My reply: To avoid yourself (kids), speaks of low self-esteem.

A wise man once told me, and I think it applies here, "There is always a reason, but never an excuse." We need to be available, fellas. Work it out, do what you must, but make sure the next generation has the benefit of your guidance, your presence, care, and love.

Day 252
"Prayer is entering communion with God. It is sharing our intimate thoughts and feelings about our experiences and getting God's input."
– Dr. A.R. Bernard, Christian Cultural Center

Day 253
Recognize your truth. It's the power of your journey. Our personal history is often filled with things we like to forget. We are confronted with hurt, shame, guilt, and regret, as well as victory and triumph.

Acknowledge it all because it speaks to the goodness of God in your life.

Day 254
Life happens in time.

Day 255
"There are no overnight success stories with long lasting results. There are "meteoric rises" & super suddenly stories after years & tears & hard work. Most quietly conquer the early chapters. Then BOOM! It'll look like a surprise to some – most of all the haters! Keep grinding!"
     - Andrienne Bankert, TV host, award-winning journalist, and actor

Day 256
AMBER Alerts: AMBER Alerts are emergency messages issued when a law enforcement agency determines a child has been abducted and is in imminent danger. These alerts galvanize communities to assist in the search for and safe recovery of an abducted child. The alerts are broadcast through radio, TV, road signs, cell phones, and other data-enabled devices.

We all get these notices. Initially, I would turn off the notice without giving much attention to the message. I don't remember when that changed, but I now respond by stopping and praying for the health, safety, and well-being of the children. I may not always be able to pull away, but I make a concerted effort to pray. I would encourage you to do the same.

We all have an internal system that alerts us to focus. It might be a recurring thought you ponder from time to time or a feeling of uneasiness about a situation or setting. Your body gives you hints that you need to get rest or attend to something that has been ailing you. Practice listening to your inner self/your spirit/your conscious, and your body.

I don't always understand the message or why I feel a certain way, but I try to quiet myself, pray, and ask God for understanding. How many people felt uneasy or a strain in their body and decided to seek medical help only to find out they avoided a more serious medical condition. Equally important is your ability to show compassion or concern for others when you notice something different about them. You may ask, "How are you doing?" or "Are you okay?" You may decide not to inquiry directly but pray for them at a different time.

With so many vying issues, voices, and concerns, it may be difficult to cut through all the distractions. Nevertheless, it is important to slow down enough to listen and respond to external and internal alerts.

Do you want to be more attentive in your life? Ask God about it.

"Trust in the Lord with all your heart, and lean not on your own understanding; In all your ways acknowledge Him, And He shall direct your paths." Proverbs 3:5-6 (NKJV)

Day 257
I discussed hope with my barber—hoping to walk my daughter down the aisle, hoping to play basketball with my grandkids, hoping to enjoy a nice meal with family and friends, hoping to walk my property for hours, and hoping to keep, nurture, and protect hope. Don't give up hope.

Day 258
Who do you represent?

We wear team jerseys and hats. We call ourselves the _____eans, just put your hometown in front. We belong to this group or that group. More than the outer facade, your representation is comprised of your thoughts and behaviors. I want to represent love.

Your representation is not just a thought, it must be followed and proven by actions. I said I want to represent love, but if I am unlovely, mean, rude, and spiteful, those behaviors do not represent love. If you asked people who know me, my colleagues, friends, and family members, they should be able to attest to my character and representation. They should be able to verify it.

I know I have a long way to go, but for me, love is the gold standard. Read 1 Corinthians 13:1-7 (NIV):

"If I speak in the tongues of men or of angels, but do not have love, I am only a resounding gong or a clanging cymbal. ² If I have the gift of prophecy and can fathom all mysteries and all knowledge, and if I have a faith that can move mountains, but do not have love, I am nothing. ³ If I give all I possess to the poor and give over my body to hardship that I may boast, but do not have love, I gain nothing.

⁴ Love is patient, love is kind. It does not envy, it does not boast, it is not proud. ⁵ It does not dishonor others, it is not self-seeking, it is not easily angered, it keeps no record of wrongs. ⁶ Love does not delight in evil but rejoices with the truth. ⁷ It always protects, always trusts, always hopes, always perseveres."

Based on this definition of love, I have a lifetime of work and personal improvement ahead of me. How about you?

What do you represent or want to represent? Why?

_____

_____

_____

Day 259

I have not been to Africa yet. I have not been to Australia yet. I have not been to Italy yet. I have not been to Paris. I have not been to Egypt. I have not been to Israel. I have not been to Napa Valley. I'm looking forward to it all. Please share what's next for you.

_____

_____

Day 260

It's me. Have you ever been upset over a situation and pointed the finger at yourself? Example. I have to work on being more patient or maybe I am taking the wrong approach in this matter. It's not always the other person. Sometimes it's us. It's me.

Day 261

TV, the electronic device that brings shows, movies, sporting events, and infomercials into your living room. In fact, we have so many choices and cable stations it is customary to have 100 plus channels to choose from not including the apps that bring even more entertainment in our homes. You now can get caught up with your favorite show or binge watch every episode available. Great right?

That question is debatable. My grandfather use to call the TV, the "Idiot Box." Business Consultant and Wealth Creation Guru Myron Golden calls it the "Income Reducing Device." I tend to agree that aimless, unscheduled tv watching is counterproductive. Remember, when you say yes to something, you are saying no to something else. I don't know about you, but I have a real need to get information to benefit my life, learn a new skill, earn more, and think differently.

I have become strategic in my viewing choices. The television is used as a teaching device or reward after completing a task. I can no longer afford to waste time and become mesmerized and infatuated with someone else's "reality." I want to win! How about you?

Day 262

He sees that. That thing you do when there is only you and no audience. It's a good thing that comes with a promise. What you do in secret for God and for goodness, He will reward in the open. Carry on.

Reference: Matthew 6:1-4 (NKJV)

Day 263

Check Yourself.

C'mon O, you're buggin'. Hold up, partner. Sometimes you got to check yourself. It is highly recommended. When you humble yourself, you qualify for promotion.

Sitting at a computer terminal, my co-workers and I would work out issues and problems by having a self-dialogue or talking through a problem. Don't tell me I am the only one who discusses issues or asks questions out loud. In fact, I used to joke about it.

You can talk to yourself, and I think many people do. It becomes a big question mark when you argue with yourself. That's when folks will debate on facilitating an intervention on your behalf. In all seriousness, being able to critique yourself in a constructive manner can lead to greater development and learning. Keeping yourself grounded or levelheaded will help you avoid pitfalls.

How do you check/critique yourself?

Reference: 1 Peter 5:6

Day 264
Here. Here. Here. Absent. Here. Here. Here. Absent. Here. Smalls: PRESENT! I said, present most of the time in school. I encourage you to say and be present in your life. Be PRESENT.

Day 265
TEAM.

Team is for the journey. Team is for the battle. Team is for the struggle. Team is for the comeback after a loss. Team is for the win, whether a blowout victory or last-second field goal. Team helps to carry the load. Seriously, who is on your team?

List three people you consider teammates. These individuals are trustworthy, give honest feedback, and hold you accountable.

1.

2.

3.

Do you have the right team? Who do you need to add, bench, or trade?

Day 266

Gratitude going deeper. Being grateful for my life in a "keeping up with Joneses society." We often compare ourselves with others. Be careful! Your next level depends on you taking what you have been given, acknowledging the giver (God), and doing your very best. Stay focused.

Day 267

Then God said, "Let there be light, and there was light." Genesis 1:3 (NKJV).

Recognize when you say and proclaim, "Let there be light," you are saying, "Let there be life." Light is required for life. When you are awakened to the Truth of God's Word, you are enlivened.

Day 268

God is so generous and long-suffering. He allows us to learn, making our own decisions and deciding that our best choice is trusting Him, and acknowledging we need Him.

Day 269

Yes! Yes you can go when the light turns green. We all want it now. Sometimes the hardest thing to do is wait for it. The delay is not a no, it just might not be the time for it. Perhaps you have to learn something while you wait. Think about the analogy of the stop light.

Is there an area in your life that feels like a red light? Please explain.

Barring any equipment malfunction, being at a red light means that the light will soon turn green. It may be necessary and beneficial to express your displeasure. However, don't lose patience now, you're almost home. Television and film mogul Tyler Perry said, "It doesn't matter if a million people tell you what you can't do or if 10 million people tell you no, if you get one Yes from God, that is all you need."

Day 270
Quiet Time.

Use part of the day to unplug, unwind, and meditate or just do some deep breathing in silence. There are many benefits to silence. A recent article by the WhisperRoom, listed 7 Benefits of Silence. See excerpts below.[26]

1. **Silence helps you concentrate**. A silent environment or one with just a little background noise will help you concentrate the best.

2. **Silence and creativity**. Many great scientists like Albert Einstein and Sir Isaac Newton worked with little to no outside interference. Psychoanalyst Ester Buchholz previously explained the best creative work is often completed in solitude or after a period of solitude.

3. **Awareness is achieved through silence**. Distractions can hamper your ability to attend.

4. **Silence provides you with a sense of calm**. A period of silence each day allows you the chance to relax and reduce stress levels.

5. **Noise has been linked to a lower level of learning**. UPMC Health has reported a link between the levels of noise a child is exposed to with their abilities as a student. The more noise a child is exposed to, the worse they perform at school and the harder they find the concentration levels to work with. In the 21st-century, the exposure of children to tablets, cell phones, and video games has increased the level of hearing impairment which affects their ability to learn and develop correctly.

6. **Productivity and silence.** In an article by Inc., research[27] suggests that doing nothing and remaining silent has been reported to increase the production of new brain cells which could make you more productive in the future simply by doing nothing. Taking time to daydream may actually improve your productivity tenfold.

7. **Silence gives you more patience**. Learning to enjoy silence cultivates calmness and peacefulness. When regularly practiced, your tolerance levels for becoming impatient will likely grow, too.

Give it a try. Find a place where you can avoid noise. Spend three minutes in silence. You might close your eyes and breathe deeply. Just begin to quiet yourself.

Try to expand the time to five, ten, or fifteen minutes. Find a bench outside and just sit down without music in your ears. Listen to the wind or the sound of birds chirping. Discover the benefits of silence and pass it on.

How long did you keep silent?

What was your experience doing this exercise?

_____

_____

Day 271

I'm not eating those three slices. Had the taste for pizza. Went to the shop, where two ladies ate lunch. I ordered three slices, silence. I blurted out, "These three slices are not all for me." Laughter followed with some mid-day pleasantries. "Have a nice day, ladies." The End.

Day 272

I heard it said, faith is blind. I don't think so. Faith is seeing it, having it, receiving it, believing it, and working and moving toward it.

Day 273

When I cook, the first ingredient I use is love. Love is the first and main ingredient.

Day 274

Saddened by continued violence. What effects one, affects us all. Let's check up and in with the next generation. We need more community fathers and mothers, uncles and aunties, big brothers and big sisters. They don't know the way; they need us, and we need them. Let's restore our families and communities by acknowledging our needs and fulfilling and appreciating our roles.

Day 275
Who do you follow? Think about it.

Day 276
Relationships.

If you were going on a long road trip, someone must drive. Now both people can drive, but one at a time. What would happen if the man and the woman struggled to grab the steering wheel? You guessed it, catastrophe. I have a solution. One person drives and the other provides company, conversation, direction. At a rest stop, both parties decide to switch. Wow! What you know, they arrive at their destination, safe, refreshed, and perhaps a little closer...and then a little closer.

Day 277
"Curious" by Midnight Star.

While outside enjoying the summer weather with my daughter, listening to music by the fire pit, the song "Curious" by Midnight Star played. The song's chorus said, "Curiosity never hurt nobody, I'm curious."
My daughter took exception to this lyric, "No Daddy, he's wrong, curiosity killed the cat!" I pondered her reaction to the song and decided to dig a little deeper. You may have heard the expression, "curiosity killed the cat." This proverb is used to warn of the dangers of unnecessary investigation or experimentation. She was right.

Curiosity can be a virtue; however, it can be dangerous as well. How many people are hooked on drugs because they were curious? How many marriages have been destroyed because someone was curious about an affair? How many people have been hurt or even killed because of hazardous activities?

Please understand I am making a distinction between healthy curiosity that spurs development, learning, and growth from curiosity that is unnecessary. In my opinion, curiosity becomes unnecessary when the results are known and negative, or the risk greatly outweighs the reward. Think about it.

What are you curious about?

_____

_____

Is your curiosity healthy? Why or why not?

_____

_____

Day 278
Are you preparing for rain?

Rain is necessary for growth. Farmers anticipate rainfall for the season and decide what types of crops to plant. Sometimes rain is problematic in that it inundates the soil, causes erosion, and makes harvesting difficult.

Rain does not adapt to us; we adapt to it. We dress appropriately, carry umbrellas, and turn on windshield wipers. Rain gives life by replenishing reservoirs, waterways, forests, and jungles. It also causes flash flooding, and dangerous landslides. Precipitation and wetting rains can help quell or slow wildfires.

Rain improves air quality by collecting airborne particles such as soot, smoke, and dust, bringing them to the ground. There is something refreshing about experiencing a summer rain or the brisk, clean aftermath.

Whether a little or a lot, rain is on its way.

Are you preparing for the rain? Are you sowing seeds in your life that will germinate once the rain falls? Are you developing strategies and competencies required to withstand the storms of life?

If you answered no to any of these questions, please reconsider your stance and prepare for rain.

Day 279
"Whatcha See Is Whatcha Get." That was the title of a song by The Dramatics. It is a profound statement. What you see is indeed what you get. Here it is, what you see is based on what you think. I think possibility, I think prosperity, I think promise. What do you see?

Day 280
"Get over it!"
> *— Pastor Ray Hadjstylianos, Living Word Christian Church*

The phrase "to get over it!" does not mean, by doing so, the hurt will go away or the memory of the betrayal will suddenly vanish. But you must resolve that you, with the help of the Lord, will get over it, that it will no longer hold you and your destiny captive.

When I heard Pastor Ray say these words, for me it was a shaking, an encouragement to snap out of it. It's a belief in the untapped power of God in your life to overcome circumstances and trials. It's a coach yelling, "C'mon you can do it."

Day 281
Relationships: I talk to ladies and they say, "O, it's rough out there." I talk to guys and they say, "O, it's rough out there." What's going on y'all? I got to talk about it on my show, Kicking It with Brother Smalls, www.brothersmalls.com. Please let me know if you believe relationships" is an important topic. Comment at info@brothersmalls.com.

Why is it so difficult for people to find someone to vibe (connect) with in a real and meaningful way?

_____

_____

_____

Can understanding wants vs. needs play a factor? Why or why not?

Day 282

Greatness involves consistency. If you can commit to being consistent, you are on the road to greatness.

Day 283

Each one reach one. I encourage you today, as you get yours, recognize that your getting is not only for you, but for others, too. Share your blessing with someone else.

Day 284

I'd be a fool to ever change. If she said she loves the way I am. Song: "Forever, for Always, for Love" by Luther Vandross.

Day 285

Experiment: Play Pharrell Williams, "Happy."

Day 286

REWIND. Sometimes we play back things that don't propel us forward. I want to encourage myself and others to use the lessons of the past to pave a brighter future. I don't know about you, but I want my life to be filled with graduations.

Day 287

"As the deer pants for the water brooks, So pants my soul for You, O God." Psalm 42:1 (NKJV).

My challenge, and I imagine the challenge of others, is to carve out quiet time, times of solace and silence.

Day 288

I said too much. I apologize.

When was the last time you had to apologize because you said too much?

Day 289

Every heartbeat is grace. Every heartbeat is grace. Every heartbeat is grace...Cherish life.

Day 290

"Keep your heart with all diligence for out of it flows the issues of life." Proverbs 4:23 (NKJV)

Be deliberate today in guarding and watching over what you allow to enter your mind. Let the promises of God permeate your thinking, be preeminent, first, and central in your thoughts.

Day 291

If you are having difficulty with a situation or a relationship. Ask yourself if you are trying to help or are you trying to control.

Observation. We are created to help one another, not to control one another. In life and in relationships, if one seeks to control the other, there will be continual conflict and strife. Conversely, if we seek to submit to God, then we can submit one to another. Submission is an act of the will. I'm not forced to submit; I choose to submit. The life of submission is a life of freedom that yields peace and blessings.

Day 292

Throwing grass seed on the lawn with my bare hands, my neighbor who is a retired nurse said, "Don't do that, use a container." I knew I should use gloves or a device to seed but I was cutting corners. I appreciate that she cared enough to say something. Let's all care. Thank you Ms.Lillieth.

Day 293

Let Your Word flow into my mind and heart, Lord, and let it seep continuously out of my life. I want to exude Your essence and reflect Your glory.

Day 294

I thank you. I praise you. I pray this or that. I proclaim this or that. I purpose to do this or that. Interesting and very powerful. God has given us authority to change our lives through thoughts, words, and actions.

Day 295

In the middle of the word sin is I.

Personally, I find that when I am overly focused on my world to the point that I don't make room for others, it makes me more susceptible to sin. And what is sin? Sin is defined as an immoral act considered to be a transgression against divine law. Example: You think your neighbor's husband or wife is attractive, and you begin desiring to be with them intimately. In many cultures and religions that would be considered sinful. Whether you act on your thoughts and get involved in an extra-marital affair, the situation was cultivated by your focus on your desires.

I think it is healthy to focus intently on something you want and reach for your goals, but when your focus overrides divine law (goodness), then it is problematic. You want a position at the company, and you work hard for it. However, it is not happening fast enough for you, so you lie, cheat, and sabotage your co-workers in pursuit of your desire. Whether or not you obtain the coveted position, you have changed the composition and complexion of who you are. Think about it.

Day 296

The Caleb Plan

Father time is undefeated. You may have heard this term to describe an athlete, performer, or professional who begins to show the signs of age. They are a little slower, cannot hit or sustain the high note, nor exhibit the passion, fervor, and endurance they once did.

I can remember playing basketball with my sons. Game after game after game, I let them have it. My intention was to make them work, scrap, and earn it; I was not going to give it away. The shift seemingly happened overnight as they got bigger, stronger, and faster. It took me longer to lather up and get loose. I noticed I didn't have the same lift or quickness to the hoop. Lock-down defense and dynamic offensive plays were sporadic at best. It finally happened. They had earned it and eclipsed their dad on the court. I can still be on the court with them, but long gone are the days of total domination.

The process of getting older is a part of life. My brother, Marc, would say something similar when people mentioned the obvious during his birthday, "You're getting older." His response is classic and true, "Isn't that the goal!" I would say yes. If you are not getting older then you don't have life. Be that as it may, how we age is something we should value. We should acknowledge our age, but not surrender because of it.

We surrender to age when we give up on our hopes and dreams. We surrender when our conversation regarding our age is used as a crutch. We surrender when we fail to see the opportunities afforded by time. Joshua 14: 7-11, illustrates a model in my opinion, the Caleb Plan.

Caleb at forty years old was one of the twelve spies sent out by Moses in the Old Testament. Only he and Joshua came back with a good and encouraging report. Because of their courage and trust in God, Moses spoke blessing over them, declaring they would see and enter the Promised Land. Fast forward some forty-five years later, Caleb is now eighty-five years old, and the time of promise is upon him.

Caleb does not relinquish his hope and determination because of his age. In fact, the fire and commitment still burn brightly on the inside. In verses 10 and 11 he explains, *"And now, behold, the Lord has kept me alive, as He said, these forty-five years, ever since the Lord spoke this word to Moses while Israel wandered in the wilderness; and now, here I am this day, eighty-five years old. [11] As yet I am as strong this day as on the day that Moses sent me; just as my strength was then, so now is my strength for war, both for going out and for coming in."* Joshua 14:10-11 (NKJV)

Wow. He affirms his tenacity, strength, vigor, and vitality to realize the vision, promise, and purpose for his life. I believe Caleb had to actively maintain his mind, body, and spirit those forty-five years between the promise and the realization of the promise. It is truly a great model to follow. Recognize your age and adjust your activities to maintain your strength, mentality, hope, and vision. I'm on the Caleb Plan. How about you? Do you use your age as a crutch?

Please list the activities that you would like to pursue once more.

_____

_____

Determine whether you need to adjust your goals, or the methods used in pursuit of your goals.

Day 297

Thank you, Chadwick Boseman for bringing your vibrant talent to the big screen. I am profoundly sad over your passing and am grateful to have witnessed your brilliance. May your life continue to speak for generations to come. Sincere condolences to your loved ones. Grace and Peace.

Day 298

Decisions are powerful, they can lock or unlock so many things in your life. Decisions can propel you or thwart your progress toward your goals and destiny. The beautiful thing in God is that, if you have breath, you have an opportunity to make the right decision toward life.

Day 299

She doesn't know. I'm creating that smooth playlist for the right moment. Do a little extra today to say I love you.

Sometimes we can get stuck in a routine. I noticed my relationship was on automatic and in need of spice (variety). So, I planned a beautiful evening out with the Mrs., took her to her favorite restaurant, and during the drive, played some classic soul and rhythm and blues. Another occasion, I took off from work and surprised her by personally delivering flowers to her job. Whatever you do, be deliberate and intentional. Let your gesture say loud and clear, I LOVE YOU.

Day 300

"Power is best managed when entrusted to those who want only what God wants."

— Bishop Reford Mott, Generations Church

Day 301

This is the day the Lord has made; We will rejoice and be glad in it. Psalm 118:24 (NKJV). Be thankful. Spend some time today to think about all the things you are grateful and thankful for.

Day 302

#Setsof50

This year I turn fifty years old. To some fifty is old, and to others fifty is young. I feel like I'm just getting started. Well, not really. I've experienced a lot, but there is so much more to learn, discover, and achieve.

There are books I have not yet written and businesses I have not yet established. Properties and land to acquire and cultivate. Thoughts to express and beauty to behold. Places to visit, people to meet, and foods to enjoy.

Kids and grandkids to hug and kiss, and love to dispense. Weddings, anniversaries, births, recognitions, and celebrations of life. These fifty years have taught me to appreciate every moment…to live and love on purpose. Say I love you today. Let go of the bitterness today. Pursue peace today.

The hashtag #Setsof50 is not a workout, more of a mindset. To live life in sets of fifty is an idea to live well. As I near the milestone of reaching my first fifty, I'm encouraged to use the lessons learned and investments made to make my next fifty exceptional. How about you?

Determine today to live your best life in #Setsof50.

Day 303

It has been a journey.

In our instant society we often look at those who have achieved a level of distinction or notoriety without appreciating the journey. We think of the overnight success. The term overnight success is overused and is a misnomer. When someone is discovered or gets their big break, it is usually the result of years of hard work, dedication, and opportunity readiness. The individual prepared him/herself, and when the opportunity presented itself, they were able to take full advantage of it.

I'm concerned our young people have a concept of wealth and success that does not incorporate hard work, dedication, and consistency. They see the flash and the followers and are sidetracked into thinking that success happens overnight. Even worse is the idea that wealth and success is the accumulation of material things. Many people in this camp fall apart when they lose their toys, position, or status.

Another problem that instant gratification thinking uncovers is the unwillingness to start somewhere. People don't want to take the entry-level job. No, give me the corner suite with the panoramic view please. I had a bit of this attitude when I got my first municipal management position. I recall talking to a friend in the barber shop. I was in my first or second year on the job. As I explained my role and my desire for advancement with an air of entitlement, the brother quickly said, "You just got there, bro." His response was exactly what I needed to hear. He was right, I had just gotten there and had not yet had the time and opportunity to show my skill, aptitude, temperament, and consistency. These traits are extremely important, especially in leadership positions and are revealed through time and testing.

*"In all labor there is profit, but idle **chatter** leads only to poverty."*
Proverbs 14:23 (NKJV)

Chatter can be activities that don't help you achieve your goals and objectives, time wasters. You name it, nowadays there are so many distractions. Just look at people walking the streets. They are so busy texting or looking at their devices, that they barely notice almost clipping an elderly person or nearly causing an accident. C'mon folks, wake up.

In all seriousness, all work, indeed, is profitable. I often share this truth when talking to young people. I explain it this way: if I worked at a fast-food restaurant I would learn customer service, timeliness, collaboration, and communication skills, all while earning money. I would also learn what appeals to me, what I like or dislike. In this example, perhaps I love the atmosphere and desire to learn the various jobs in the store on a management track. Perhaps I take note of the number of customers and determine that franchise ownership is something worth pursuing. Maybe, the experience reveals I can't stand the smell of fries. In that case, I'd be looking for another job.

All these lessons and many more are gained through work, and they prepare you for your next level. You may also encounter people who can help you advance in your career. Recognize and appreciate the journey one step at a time. Let's get to work.

I mentioned success, and wealth…I believe those terms need to be defined by you. Below is my definition of success and wealth. Spend time thinking about what success and wealth mean to you.

I believe success is living out your God-designed purpose. What that means is you are uniquely gifted by God. When you tap into what makes you special and unique and live that out to the fullest while acknowledging God, you are successful.

Wealth is an all-encompassing state of peace and prosperity of mind, body, and spirit. It touches every area of your life, health, finances, social and professional relationships, family, and community.

What does success and wealth mean to you?

_____

_____

_____

Day 304
Use social media, don't let social media use you.

How many times do you pick up your phone? A study in 2019 conducted by Asurion found that within a two-year period, our smartphone dependency grew 20 percent.[28] According to the study, Americans check their cell phones ninety-six times a day, which is once every ten minutes. That number is double among young people ages eighteen to twenty-four.

A *Forbes Magazine* article[29] by Peter Suciu indicated that in 2020, Americans spent more than 1300 hours on social media. Members of Generation Z (Ages 6-24) spent a whopping nine hours a day on screen time. That fact is plausible as a result of remote learning due to the pandemic and health and safety protocols.

Increased screen time can impact sleep patterns and may lead to a less active lifestyle, weight gain, and other issues. Conversely, use of technology can aid in creating order and balance in your life. It's all in how you use it. Consider the amount of your daily screen time. Perhaps your use of technology has not necessarily increased. Instead of TV, you watch YouTube videos on your phone.

I asked my ten-year-old whether she liked playing games with her friends online or playing with her friends in person. Without hesitation, she answered in person. "I'd rather hang out with my friends." Her response was encouraging and mirrors my sentiments exactly. I enjoy reading entries online and seeing photos of friends and their loved ones, but it doesn't come close to sharing special moments with them in person. Think about it.

How much time do you spend on social media per day?

   a.   1 hour

   b.   2 hours

   c.   3 hours

   d.   4 hours

Do you think you spend too much time on social media?
If yes, how will you adjust your behavior?

_____
_____
_____

What activity or goal could you pursue instead of using social media?

Day 305
VOTE

Day 306
Global Community

When tragedy happens across the country or across the world, are you moved with compassion? I am not sure if you remember the young soccer team in 2018 that went on a cave excursion in Thailand and were trapped by rising flood waters in the Tham Luang cave system. As the waters rose, the boys had to go deeper and deeper into the cave. They were trapped for nine days, and survived by staying together, and drinking moisture dripping from the cave walls. The boys used meditation techniques taught to them by their Coach Ake, who was also stranded.

Outside the cave, the country assembled an elite Navy Seal Team, the national police, and other rescue teams. The cave rescue became an international story and effort. Many countries supported the rescue effort including US Air Force rescue specialists and cave divers from Australia, Scandinavia, Belgium, and the United Kingdom.

While the authorities raced feverishly to rescue the team, the country held national vigils for the boys. Prayer groups were formed to pray for their safe return. As a believer and parent, I also joined my faith with the faith of others. The nightmarish thought of those young men trapped in a dark cave compelled me to pray.

The boys were finally discovered by British divers John Volanthen and Rick Stanton. The elation could be felt throughout Thailand and around the world. Unfortunately, during the rescue operation, a volunteer and former Navy Seal diver, Saman Gunan, died while delivering air tanks to the boys. He lost consciousness and could not be revived. Gunan was thirty-eight years old. I share this story as a reminder that we are all connected.

I recall a discussion I had with Pastor Dimas Salaberrios of Infinity Bible Church and Director of the documentary, Chicago: America's Hidden War. I asked him about his motivation to serve in chaotic settings. He responded that his service outreach to Haiti after the devastating earthquake in 2010 proved to him that the Earth is not as big as we make it out to be. He tells a story of transporting the injured and providing aid to severely wounded people. His desire is for people to care and be empathic to the plight of others. I couldn't agree more.

We cannot lose nor neglect our connection with our fellow man. The uprising, violence, and unrest in this country, and other parts of the world should move us toward action. I am glad to be a world citizen and have participated in empowerment and relief efforts here and around the globe. I believe we must think globally and act locally. But I also believe in thinking locally and acting globally. How about you?

Day 307
You Make It

You make things better, not the other way around. Our society puts value on inanimate things at the expense of what is truly important, the person and community. We are bombarded with ads that sell us on clothes, footwear, cars, and everything in between. Some people are so enthralled with things that their entire self-worth is wrapped up in their possessions. These individuals have a difficult time when they lose their possessions. I believe these people are more prone to commit crimes against humanity when their "status" is "threatened."

We are all susceptible to this temptation. Have you ever spent more money than you could afford during the holiday season or lost the significance/meaning because your focus was misplaced? During the holiday season and all year round, it is important to acknowledge what is important. The connection between family and friends. The ability to leave an inheritance for your children's children. The sense and obligation of appreciating and being concerned with others in your family, community, and world.

The shoes don't make you; you make the shoes. The dress or suit does not make you, but you make it. The car is a means of transportation, not a reflection of your net worth, IQ, or value as a person. The group or organization is better because of your presence and involvement. I like nice things, but more importantly I want to model the proper order and perspective for our children. We have to mirror behaviors that tell them loud and clear that they are valuable, they are special, and they make the difference.

Day 308

Do you want to be more efficient and effective? Do you want to take advantage of the day? Pray.

Day 309

"You don't change until conception."

– Myles Munroe

Day 310

Raise Your Consciousness. You can raise your level of awareness in life by Attending, Hearing, and Doing (AHD).

To attend is to be present, deal with, see to, manage, and address a given situation. When you attend to something, you acknowledge it and focus on it. Hearing is super important to raising your consciousness. Hearing requires you to listen, be observant, inquire, and investigate. When you determine to hear from others, you recognize they can add something to your life. It's also a way to admit you don't have all the answers. This humble approach leads to increased learning.

Doing is where the rubber meets the road. It is no good to attend or acknowledge a situation, increase comprehension by hearing, and fail to implement what you know to do. We sometimes stall at the doing phase because we prefer convenience or comfort. Although, we may not be satisfied in our current environment, we are familiar with it.

To gain the strength to break out of convenience, you may need to remind yourself why it is necessary to raise your consciousness and get to your next level. Go back to attending, and hearing. Perhaps you can find a friend who does what you want to do and can hold you

accountable. Try this prayer as well, "Lord help me to do XY or Z."
Be as specific as possible when identifying the issues you are dealing
with.

We must raise our consciousness because our thinking is directly
aligned with our doing. *"As a man thinks in his heart (mind), so is he,"*
Proverbs 23:7 (NKJV). There are limitless applications and levels to
raising your conscientiousness and awareness. You can become more
health conscious, wealth conscious, love conscious, and self-aware.

As we live, hopefully we learn more about ourselves and others for our
collective benefit as a society. Attend, hear, and then do. Raise your
consciousness.

Day 311
*With a little faith (belief in action), you can move mountains. Belief
only is not enough. Action without direction can be hazardous. When
you combine both belief and action, you're activating faith which
pleases God and makes all things possible.*

Day 312
*Counteract negative conditioning in your life by actively pursuing
knowledge and wisdom. A great place to start is by acknowledging
God.*
Reference: Proverbs 1:7

Day 313
I love y'all. I have to follow up love with love. John 3:16

Day 314
It's okay.

You and I are the same, yet we are different. We are both members of
the human race and world family, but we are on separate journeys. At
times our paths will be aligned, and other times on divergent tracks.
It's okay.

I believe there is a freedom and peace when we decide to follow our God-given path and destiny. Some will not understand, but it's okay. I remember in high school working out while others were going out. My focus was on preparing my body to compete. As I jogged past people hanging out, I felt like the work would pay off, and it did. I was able to make both the football and basketball teams in high school.

The late great Kobe Bryant was an exceptional athlete, with an even greater work ethic. Many of the NBA greats attest to his drive and will to win. His regiment included strenuous workouts before and after team workouts, study of great players, and film sessions. His dedication elevated his game and mentality. He was special. He was different. He accepted his track and giftings and worked tirelessly to maximize them.

There is a tradeoff to putting all your focus in attention into an endeavor, job, or business. Whether you give it thirty-, sixty-, or ninety-nine-point nine percent, it all depends on what is important to you, what you value. Because we are different, we will appropriate varying levels of effort to a myriad of pursuits and initiatives, and it's okay.

Give yourself room to grow as you home in on your special giftings and talent.

Day 315
I'm encouraged like never before to live and share my faith.

I will not, however, allow unbelievers to define what it is to be a Christian. The Bible says, "For God so love the world that He gave His only begotten Son, that whoever believes in Him should not perish but have everlasting life John 3:16" (NKJV). The Bible also says, "You shall love your neighbor as yourself" Mark 12:31 (NKJV).

I would hope you would love someone enough to tell them the truth, "Hey man, you had too much to drink, let me drive you home." I resolve today to live out my faith by loving people and sharing the life-giving Gospel of Jesus Christ. I resolve today to love my neighbor as myself, and I resolve to be a truth teller no matter what. I have a right to believe, just like everybody else. Don't allow others to frame your beliefs into their box, you have a right to believe.

Day 316

Fear can be healthy if it aids you in avoiding dangerous situations/activities. Fear is unhealthy when it is used to imprison people psychologically or causes you to refrain from activities you would otherwise benefit from and enjoy. Please recognize those who are professional fear mongers.

Day 317

Who do you think you are?

Sometimes that question is posed by others, and sometimes we ask ourselves.
But who do you think you are to believe that you can accomplish and achieve success, open your own business, graduate college, live debt free, liberate your thinking, find love, and strengthen your body? Very often this question comes in mid-stream of our pursuit of these things. It's a challenging thought that can slow your progress if you let it. Questions like this require a response. If left unchecked they can be corrosive and counterproductive. I AM A CHILD OF GOD. Yes, you can choose words that remind you of your purpose, power, and privilege. The next time you hear words that question your ability, your vision, and your promise, respond by saying, "I AM A CHILD OF GOD."

Day 318

I Apologize.

To apologize is to express regret for something done wrong. We're not perfect, we get it wrong a lot. Well, let me speak for myself. I know I do. If we're not perfect and we mess up often, why is it so hard for us to say I'm sorry, I apologize, my bad? We find it difficult to talk about our shortcomings. I think if we confessed our wrongs to one another in love more often, we would live healthier, freer, and productive lives.

Not apologizing is akin to leaving things unresolved. Living with the weight of unresolved issues can impact every area of your life, especially relationships. In a webpage article at oureverydaylife.com[30], Sam Grover explains, the emotional effects from having unresolved issues in a relationship can manifest through external blame, self-deception, boiling over, and a lack of closeness.

External blame is attributing someone or something with your negative feelings when it is really caused by an unresolved issue of the past. Self-deception occurs when you try to ignore an issue. Dealing with an issue can provide self-learning and growth, but personal development is forfeited if you're unwilling to deal with the matter. If you don't learn yourself, it makes it harder to learn and understand others.

Boiling over is just that—either you or your partner becomes fed up with behaviors caused by unresolved issues. This may cause irrevocable damage and/or break up of the relationship. Lastly, closeness in relationships is forged over time and experience. Unresolved issues in a relationship can drive a wedge between partners.

I'm convinced it is better to be honest with yourself and confess your faults than ignoring the issues and hoping they magically go away. No time like the present. I would like to apologize to everyone I have slighted, let down, or neglected. I imagine there are things I've done growing up and as a man that I am totally unaware of, as well as people I have offended who are still carrying the offense. To those individuals, please hear my heart. I sincerely apologize for any hurt I have caused.

As amazing as this dynamic can be, the Scriptures give a more powerful word than apology, and that word is repentance. Repentance is stronger because it acknowledges wrong and determines to move in the opposite direction. When you repent of something, you express your regret and actively behave in ways that counteract the offensive action. Repentance also acknowledges God as the source of strength to combat negative and harmful tendencies, while embracing that which is good.

There is a need for us to apologize to one another when we fall short. This concept can strengthen relationships and foster self-development and growth. Also, when we recognize our faults and repent to God, we are released from the burden of unforgiveness. 1 John 1:9 (NKJV) says, *"If we confess our sins, He is faithful and just to forgive us our sins and to cleanse us from all unrighteousness."*

Apologizing is not being cowardly but taking corrective action to move forward in your life. Repenting is an acknowledgement of wrong, acceptance of our frailty, and the need for God with a mentality to move away from offensive behaviors. Use both apology and repentance to facilitate self-learning, strengthen relationships, and cultivate an abundant life and lifestyle.

Day 319
24/7.

Many people wish there were more hours in a day. So much to do and so little time. Others squander time with no regard. As you know, time does not wait for anyone. Time will elapse whether you like it or not. Since time and change are absolute, I'd encourage you to take a sober approach by recognizing that today will never happen again. Pause now and write down the name of the person you have been thinking of catching up with and calling: _____.

Write down the activity you have been wanting to do: _____.

Now, thank God for your life and ask Him to help you appropriate time to accomplish the things He has put in your heart (mind).

Day 320
"The joy of the Lord is your strength." Nehemiah 8:10 (NKJV)

Day 321
"It is better to give than to receive."
Reference: Acts 20:35 (NKJV)

It is crucial we give of ourselves during this time. Give our wisdom, insight, and encouragement. We need each other to make it through, and remember by doing so we prepare for a return in our life.

Day 322
Agents and messengers of hope are being born every day. Think about it.

Babies are being born right now, giving hope, joy, and solace to so many. Be encouraged today and use your gifts to positively impact the lives of others. Grace and Peace. Facts: Worldwide, around 385,000 babies are born each day.[31]

Day 323
Bully Culture.

We live in a society that wants you to think like the masses or else. If you don't believe like I believe then you are a horrible human being. It's false, it's destructive, and it is not Godly. God gives us choice. We always have a choice. Choose life.

Day 324
At times we come short to reaching our daily goals. We do not dot every i and cross every t. Don't get discouraged. It is important we learn to pick ourselves up and get back on course. Keep pressing and move forward... Each time you do this, you learn perseverance. You're getting closer. You're getting warmer.

Day 325
Search for kindness.

Andrienne Bankert, *TV Host, award-winning journalist and actor*, during an interview[32] highlighted the importance of searching for kindness. As an assignment, her assistants and interns searched for stories illustrating kindness. She recommends bringing attention to kindness when starting meetings.

Interesting note: The people who were given the assignment to search for good stories often reported feeling better, and they thanked her for the assignment. These individuals found stories that helped them find comfort in a trying time, providing hope. These accounts are examples of a biblical truth. *"Anxiety in the heart of man causes depression, but a good word makes it glad."* Proverbs 12:25 (NKJV)

Leading with and exemplifying kindness can be a catalyst to foster a collaborative culture and more cohesive atmosphere and environment at work and home. Kindness is a powerful draw. People may not always admit it, but I don't know anyone who does not want to be treated kindly. With so much turmoil and stress in the world, kindness is sorely needed. Determine today to be an agent of change. Lead the way through kindness.

Day 326
If you don't want to get stung by bees, stay away from bees.

I heard this analogy from Pastor Corey Brooks of New Beginnings Church of Chicago. He was reciting a saying from his grandfather R.B. Haynes. Pastor Brooks used the analogy to encourage people to be mindful and wise about the people they associate with and the situations they allow themselves to get into.

This profound saying recognizes that the hearer has an understanding and knowledge of potential risks and dangers. Why is that important? Each day we see and hear signs that warn us to stop, slow down, proceed with caution, enter at our own risk, and beware, among others.

Although we often understand the risks of certain behaviors, sometimes we lack self-discipline or self-control. We enjoy the feeling and activity. Maybe it's something we do in excess or something that goes against our morals and standards.

When your focus is diverted on passion and pleasure, you can easily develop an emotional blind spot, an inability to detect and discern vulnerability. This is the danger zone. Change your perspective as soon as possible. Consider the consequences and eventual sting of your behaviors. What you sow, you will also reap (**Reference:** Galatians 6:7-9). Think about it.

Day 327

With all the commotion and turmoil of 2020 and 2021, please endeavor to exact faith for the next generation. They are depending on us to keep the faith. Massive faith is not required. In fact, God works with your best, even if your best faith is the size of a mustard seed— tiny, miniscule.

Day 328

I'd rather. Social media is fine, but it pales in comparison to hearing your voice, laughing, listening to music, grown-up conversations, breaking bread with loved ones and sharing hugs. I will be deliberate to reach out and spend quality time with others. I need more than a like.

How about you? If you don't have family or you don't have friends, start by acknowledging God. Thank Him for life, health, and strength. Thank Him for the use of your faculties. Thank Him for another day. Thank Him for employment, food on the table, and clothes on your back. Thank Him for the opportunity to give love and receive love. An attitude of gratitude is attractive.

Consider what type of relationship you want to build, and then ask the Lord Jesus Christ to help you build those qualities in yourself. Do you want a friend who is considerate? Start to be more considerate—give a bigger tip, open a door for someone, or give a cordial greeting. Do you want a friend who listens? Practice listening. Don't be so quick to tune people out when they express their points of view. Do you want a friend who is honest? Be honest with yourself, acknowledge struggles and disappointments.

Relationships, family, and community are built over time and are comprised of unique and special people. Understand your uniqueness by acknowledging God in your life.

References: Proverbs 3:5, Peter 5:5-7 (NKJV)

Day 329

You always provide. I am comforted by the fact that I am loved by God. As I ready myself to approach Him in prayer, inside I smile because I have personal knowledge and experience of His provision in my life. It's like entering a game knowing the outcome...I win. 😊

Day 330

Put a light on it.

Our mental and emotional struggles became weightier when we keep them to ourselves. Everyone needs an outlet, someone to talk to, and times of refreshing. We are all different, and what works for me may not necessarily work for you. Acknowledge God for the answer.

When you read Scriptures, you'll see that Jesus provided healing to many using different strategies and tactics. He sometimes prayed, laid hands, told someone to bathe, pronounced healing, and made a mixture using dirt. All these methods yielded the same results, healing, and restoration. Jesus also recognized the need to refuel and recharge as he often pulled away to pray and commune with God the Father.

Don't suffer in darkness. Put a light on it. Just talking about a concern to a trusted friend can be beneficial. You may find that others are dealing with or have dealt with a similar situation. Getting feedback, perhaps seeking counsel from a pastor and/or mental health professional, may also be warranted.

The focus here is to reach out and let someone know you need assistance. Seeking help is a power move and not a sign of weakness. It's wise to get counsel, especially in times of distress. Again, the exact relief and remedy will be different based on the individual and the situation and setting.

For me, putting a light on it very often means prayer and reading and reciting the Word of God. When feelings of trepidation try to creep into my thinking, I am reminded that God has not given me a spirit of fear, but of power, love, and a sound mind (**Reference:** 2 Tim. 1:7).

Sometimes getting fresh air, taking a walk, or exercise helps. I have also sought and received counseling, which was priceless.

Is there something you are struggling with that could use some light or illumination?

If so, determine how you will seek assistance and don't be discouraged if your initial attempt to access help is not met with an immediate reply. Stay with it!

Day 331

Check it out. Below are books, music, and shows worth reading, hearing, and seeing.

- Nicole Lynn, *Agent You: Show Up, Do the Work, and Succeed on Your Own Terms*
  I thoroughly enjoyed this book. The insight and recommendations were spot on.

- Shawn Rochester's books, *The Black Tax* and *CPR for the Soul*
  The action steps provided in both these books are invaluable with generational impact.

- Mike Phillips, "Taking Off the Covers"
  If you want to vibe, groove, and set the mood, listen to Mike Phillips or go to see him perform live.

- *DMI Nativity: Birth of a King*
  Artistic Director, Robert Evans. This performance is powerful and moving.

- Terri Small, "My Desire"
  I am fortunate to know Terri Small as my sister-in-law. Her songs are victorious and mirror a lifestyle I have been blessed to witness.

- *Ascended: The Omega Nexus* by Roger and Jerry Reece. Once you pick up this science fiction novel, you'll find it hard to put down. The superheroes are compelling and unique.

- *RESPECT-* The powerful and moving story of the Queen of Soul, Aretha Franklin. What an amazing film and ensemble of actors starting with Jennifer Hudson, Forest Whitaker, Marlon Wayans, Audra McDonald, Marc Maron, Tituss Burgess, and Mary J. Blige. Wow! Much Respect.

- Danica Hart, Devynn Hart, and Trea Swindle. The beautiful and talented Chapel Hart Band. If you haven't seen these ladies of country music yet, what are you waiting for?

- *Street God* by Dimas Salaberrios
  This book is a remarkable telling of the real-life story of a drug dealer whose life is miraculously turned around by the power of God.

- Documentary. "Chicago: America's Hidden War."
  Written by: Ray Moore J.R., Dimas Salaberrios, and Tiffany Salaberrios. This critically acclaimed film is powerful and gripping. I believe this film can be a catalyst for lasting change in the city of Chicago and cities across the country.

Day 332
Getting a no is sometimes a form of protection or setup for promotion. God is good all the time.

Day 333
Get dirty.

Clean up the mess. There is great value and profit in cleaning up a mess. Being willing to get your hands dirty, to exert effort toward making things better will attract people and resources.

For example, when you make an appointment or visit an attorney, doctor, mechanic, arborist, plumber, electrician, contractor, consultant, counselor, or tutor, often there is a problem (mess) you want fixed. These sought-after individuals are problem solvers, and because they can help clean up messes (problems), they are compensated handsomely. The better they are at solving problems (messes), the more valuable they become.

People who see the value of cleaning up messes are also visionaries and developers. There are plenty of HGTV shows that depict business owners who buy dilapidated properties, pay a team of professionals to renovate the property, then sell it for a profit. These individuals were not scared off by first appearances. They saw the beauty of the finished product before the contract was signed.

One person may see a field overgrown with weeds and decide to avoid the area. Another person will see the same field and think of planting crops or building a row of houses. The difference between the two individuals may be expertise, resources, and experience. However, one individual made the choice to get dirty, or understood, as they cleaned up a "mess," their reward would be increased knowledge, wisdom, and understanding.

Consider this truth by reading Proverbs 14:4 (NKJV).
"Where no oxen are, the trough is clean;
But much increase comes by the strength of an ox."

Is there something you do that makes things easier or better?

_____

_____

Do you make order out of chaos? Please explain.

_____

_____

Day 334
Belief is a gift. Ask God for the gift of belief.

Belief is very powerful and necessary for achievement and success in life. People who believe are doers. When we embark on a new initiative or challenge, we employ belief.

- I want to become an engineer, architect, writer, singer, doctor, lawyer, athlete, farmer, mechanic, truck driver.

- I want to get married.

- I want to open my own business.

- I want to get in better shape or live a healthier lifestyle.

- I want to play basketball with my grandkids.

- I want to learn a new language.

- I want to have a better relationship with my spouse.

- I want to get through the day and maintain a positive outlook.

- I want to finish an assignment on time.

- I want to visit my relatives and travel.

- I want to support my favorite charity or adopt a child.

- I want to complete this book and answer all the questions.

The list is limitless. Believing is a part of our everyday lives, from tying our shoes to walking on the moon. Your belief system and degree to which you believe directly impacts the level and quality of your life. That is why you must safeguard your thoughts, cultivate your thinking, and be careful your words line up with what you want in life.

After Jesus and His disciples fed the 5,000, the multitudes followed Jesus desiring another sign, another helping, and another meal. Jesus explained that the pursuit of everlasting food (eternal life) is more important than seeking food that perishes. He told the people that He is the bread of life, and they that come to Him would never hunger, nor thirst. He was referring to everlasting life through belief in Him.

Belief is necessary for this life and everlasting life. A life of vibrancy, and victory is available now. Ask God for the gift of belief.
Reference: John 6

Day 335

Even though you're right, God is still concerned with your heart and the way you respond. This is applicable to relations, relationships, and a host of other scenarios. Think about it.

Day 336

Great exercise. Write down three people in your life whom you are thankful for, then tell them. Example: I am thankful that you are my friend, brother, sister, mother, wife, husband, etc. Let people know with words and deeds that you appreciate them.

1.

2.

3.

Day 337

I want a President/Vice-President who will respect me enough to foster the ideal of choice.

If I don't believe what you believe, that doesn't make me a Martian. We just have a different approach/opinion. The discourse in our country has become zero-sum and ultra-polarizing. Don't condone this nonsense. Instead, speak up and speak out. Support candidates who represent your ideals, and I hope they carry an obligation to restore civility in our political discourse. What has transpired in recent years is outright embarrassing.

Day 338

Change it up.

Change the channel. Change what you're listening to. Change your workout. Change your hairstyle.

Sometimes to jump-start a shift in your life and different mindset, you have to change it up. I will take my own advice and change my presentation. Stay tuned...

Day 339
Goodness and Mercy. Psalm 23:6
Health and Wealth, Prosperity and Success, Faith and Charity, Peace and Joy.

The Word promises goodness and mercy to those shepherded by the Most High God. All the things listed above are good and denote the goodness of God. Add to the list, reflecting on your own experiences.

_____
_____
_____

Day 340
Out of debt, needs are met, plenty more to put in store!

I first heard this phrase listening to a talk given by Creflo Dollar. The saying resonated with me, and I began reciting it every time I got a mailing for additional credit cards, personal loans, or a similar solicitation to incur debt. It became a mantra and reminder to stay focus. Don't be tricked into a special deal, limited time offer, no payment/no interest until three months, six months, twelve months down the line. Usually these "deals" don't save the consumer money in the long run. You pay more interest, sales tax, and finance charges.

You may have a goal of debt-free living or being able to invest more in your future, but day after day you are inundated with these mailers. Credit card issuers maintain direct mailing campaigns because it has been proven historically to be cost effective. The credit card companies use analytics with a high degree of precision to segment and target prospective customers. It's not a bad thing in a way, these companies have determined that you're a good match for their products.

With that said, it may seem like an added chore to go through a package of mail with a half dozen credit card offers. I would encourage you to flip it. When I get one of these mailers I start to shred. While shredding, I recite my vision and goal: OUT OF DEBT, NEEDS ARE MET, PLENTY MORE TO PUT IN STORE (SAVE, INVEST, DONATE). This habit has turned an annoyance into a daily affirmation. Each time I recite the phrase, I am reminded to keep pressing toward my goals and objectives. Try it. I think you'll find it applicable in various scenarios and situations.

Day 341

Fill in the blank. I can have an excellent _____ because God is in it. Don't worry if you didn't have the best example of a relationship or aptitude in your life. When you acknowledge God and trust His guidance, you are bound to succeed.

So many people avoid relationships and activities designed for them because they've had a bad experience or a bad example. How many people have you talked to who avoid committed relationships because they were in a traumatic one or did not have a healthy example of a loving relationship when they were growing up.

Do you avoid relationships and/or activities because of a prior experience? Please explain.

_____
_____
_____

Congratulations. Identifying and describing a concern, issue, or problem is the first step in solving it or gaining the insight to learn from it. You may want to pause, pray, and/or seek advice from a trusted friend, pastor, or counselor. Take a deep breath, relax, and understand you are on the right track. One step at a time, one day at a time.

Day 342

Iron sharpens iron.

A recent message to a friend: You are my friend, and I trust if you ever had to tell me something that could hurt but was good for me, you would tell me. Can folks in your circle sharpen you?

I've heard that some, because of fame and status, don't appreciate people in their circle who can check them. I'm not certain of this, but I think it is plausible. Some people, no matter their status, have a hard time taking constructive criticism. It is important to appreciate the difference between constructive criticism and being hypercritical.

Constructive criticism is a helpful way of giving feedback that provides specific, actionable suggestions. Rather than providing general advice, constructive criticism gives specific recommendations on how to make positive improvements. Constructive criticism is clear, to the point, and easy to put into action. [33]

Hypercritical is being excessively and unreasonably critical, especially of small faults. A hypercritical person or overly critical person is actively looking for faults. This person will always have something to say, because no one is perfect. If you are looking for imperfections, you'll find them. Some folks would call these individuals "haters."

People who are genuine and can provide constructive criticism are an asset. Conversely, haters should be avoided. We all need people in our lives who can check us or give us good and honest feedback. I want to be sharpened. How about you?

Day 343
I'm looking forward to hugging you, friend. I'm looking forward to giving you a sincere and warm embrace. We're in a season of social distance, but we are to speak the things we desire. So, I speak family gatherings, friendly get-togethers, and new friendships. I speak life.

Day 344
Seven days of prayer.

In the next seven days, I will share with you excerpts of a personal prayer. The prayer mirrors the seven days of creation outlined in the Book of Genesis, Chapter 1. I share this prayer as a format and something I have used to keep focused. May it also serve as a reminder of the awesome work and plan of the Most High God. It's so amazing that God designed you and me to participate in His plan on the Earth. I sincerely hope you find this prayer useful and that it cultivates deeper times of devotion. Be blessed.

Sunday – (Day 1) God said, "Let there be light."
Pray for the salvation of your loves ones and advancing the Gospel of Jesus Christ. Let Your Kingdom come, let Your will be done over me and my family as it is in heaven. I declare heaven over my family. Let Your testimonies be the heritage in my family forever.

Day 345
Monday (Day 2)

God said, "Let there be a firmament in the midst of the waters, and let it divide the waters from the waters." Pray that God set apart His people and distinguish them for His glory. Pray for excellence and let the knowledge of wisdom be sweet to my soul.

Day 346
Tuesday (Day 3)

God said, "Let the land produce vegetation: seed-bearing plants and trees on the land that bear fruit with seed in it, according to their various kinds." Call forth the abundance of the land. Pray for opportunities and open doors with discernment to recognize value, and the fortitude and faith to realize the vision. Let the knowledge of wisdom be sweet to my soul.

Day 347
Wednesday (Day 4)

God said, "Let there be lights in the firmament of the heavens to divide the day from the night; and let them be for signs and seasons, and for days and years; and let them be for lights in the firmament of the heavens to give light on the earth"; and it was so.

I pray for discernment (keen understanding) in knowing the signs of the times and actions necessary to capitalize on opportunities. I pray for increased faith to believe the promises of God. Let the knowledge of wisdom be sweet to my soul.

I pray for the church family, that we would exercise wisdom and discernment (keen understanding) to lead and encourage people to have a deeper walk with God. That we would share the Gospel of Jesus Christ and be an example to others, praying for the needs of the church in our world.

Thank you, Lord, for the Spirit of Wisdom and Revelation, so that I may know you better. Thank you, Holy Spirit, that my eyes are enlightened in order to know the hope which You have called me and the riches of Your glorious inheritance in the saints, and Your incomparable great power toward us who believe. Thank you, Holy Spirit, for filling me with the knowledge of Your will through all spiritual wisdom and understanding. That I may live a life worthy of the Lord and may I please You in every way; bearing fruit in every good work, growing in the knowledge of God, being strengthened with all power according to His glorious might that I may have great endurance and patience while joyfully giving thanks to the Father, who qualified me to share in the inheritance of the saints in the kingdom of light.

Day 348
Thursday (Day 5)

God said, "Let the waters abound with an abundance of living creatures, and let birds fly above the earth across the face of the firmament of the heavens."

Thank God for His abundance toward us, His goodness. Let the knowledge of wisdom be sweet to my soul.

Day 349
Friday (Day 6)

God said, "Let Us make man in Our image, according to Our likeness; let them have dominion over the fish of the sea, over the birds of the air, and over the cattle, over all the earth and over every creeping thing that creeps on the earth."

Take the rightful authority to have dominion on Earth.
Prayer of possessing—Let the knowledge of wisdom be sweet to my soul. Let the same mind be in me that was in Christ Jesus. I declare that I have a plan, a generational plan. Help me to execute the plan today.

Day 350
Saturday (Day 7)

Thanksgiving. Consider your life, health, and strength. Consider all the good that you have been afforded—a roof over your head, clothes on your back, and food in your belly. Consider the endurance that allowed you to prevail in a trying time. Give thanks. Let the knowledge of wisdom be sweet to my soul. Rest in the provision and promises of God.

Day 351
Run/walk with my dog. Some people pull over to offer my dog water. C'mon, what about me? It's so funny but true. Dog owners are often known by their pet's name. Go figure?

Day 352
Okay, you have been reading the tweets and answering the questions. Are you seeing progress?

_____

_____

If so, use today to acknowledge and appreciate the steps you have taken and where you are right now. You may not be where you want to be, but you're not where you used to be. Give thanks. If you must go back, there is no shame in that. Get the lesson and get to your next level.

Day 353

Michelle Obama & Tracee Ellis Ross conversation at 2018 US of Women: a great interview with many nuggets (ideas worth keeping). Former First Lady Obama said, "Life is practicing, you have to practice who you want to become, recognize if you practice bad habits, they just don't go away."

Day 354

I was putting on a head scarf for my daughter this morning, and I hesitated. I considered another hat because I did not want her identity to be misunderstood. How abhorrent and tragic was that thought, that in the year 2020, a clothing accessory would make her susceptible to ridicule, jeering, and at worst, jeopardize her safety. This was an unusual and bizarre thought. So much so, I asked myself, where did it come from? I was reminded of a young man who simply wore a hooded sweatshirt. Rest in Peace, Trayvon Martin.

Day 355

Plant seeds of love, joy, hope, encouragement, advancement, increase...

Day 356

"You will never know where God is taking you unless you are first willing to leave where you are."
  – Dr. Tony Evans, Senior Pastor, Oak Cliff Bible Fellowship

Day 357

I love you. There is a command to love your neighbor as yourself. I consider you my neighbor. As we gear up for the holiday season, let this time be one of reflection, gratitude, and honoring one another. I appreciate the opportunity afforded to me to share with you. I smile and give God thanks for your triumphs, and victories. I pray for your comfort, peace, and power during times of struggle, strife, and loss. When you are blessed, I am joyful. Seeking to do good in 2022, and beyond. Let's go!

Day 358

Sunday Morning Prayer.

Bless the Lord and bless His holy name. We rejoice and are glad in the day that You have made.

We're excited and honored to be in Your Presence, Lord. We adore You, Father God, You are worthy of all praise. Thank You for Your awesome plan for our lives. Thank You for calling each and every one of us for this time in history. We are here on purpose and let us capture the purpose You have given our lives. Lord, some didn't wake up this morning, but You spoke life over us. You spoke wellness over us. You spoke healing over us. You spoke strength over us. Help us to live with that blessed assurance that You are our God and King. If You, Oh Lord, are for us, then who can be against us? Help us to honor the time You give us on Earth. Help us to spend our lives blessing others and giving You glory by being all we can be. Help us to run our race with grit and determination, knowing You desire excellence because You are a Good Father and give good gifts to Your children. In fact, You give wisdom to those who ask for it. So we ask for wisdom today. Let the knowledge of Your wisdom be sweet to our souls. Let the same Mind be in us that was in Christ Jesus that we might show forth Your Love and imitate Your character.

God said, "Let there be light." Let the light of Your Word cast out all fear. May we pursue the plan and purpose of our lives with confidence, knowing that He who begun a good work in us shall complete until the Day of Jesus Christ (**Reference:** Phil. 1:6). Let the Knowledge of Your wisdom be sweet to our souls.

Lord, You are not done with us. You are perfecting us, loving us, and preparing us to be a brighter light and influence in this world. Help us to be living manuals of Your love and kindness, advancing Your Kingdom in every area of our lives. We understand that we are called to put Your Word into action, to act on what we believe. We declare today that You are our priority, Lord, and as we acknowledge You in our lives, help, guide, and direct us to our place of destiny. Lord, this world needs us to fulfill our destiny, and we thank You for the church and the vision that is aligned with Yours.

Lord, You sent Your Word to heal us, to deliver us and bring us back into right relationship with You. So bless the speaker today. Let Your Word fill this place and fill our hearts, for where Your spirit is there is freedom…So we declare freedom from fear, freedom from poverty, freedom from addiction, freedom from vain thoughts and imaginations, freedom from sickness, and freedom from mental illness. We are whole today, for whom the Son set free is free indeed. LORD forgive us for not always walking in Your victory, we repent today and accept that we are more than conquerors in You and that we have the victory if we believe and act on your Holy Word. Thank You Lord for faith, and thank You Lord for this most precious time when we increase our faith by hearing Your Everlasting Word. In Jesus' name. Amen.

Day 359

God you created the map, the North, South, East, and West. I think getting your direction is a good thing. Which way should I go?

Day 360

Don't confuse or mistake the current state, condition, or circumstance of an individual with the indomitable potential inside of them. God can turn it around.

Day 361

I have many sisters but one wife.

I was in a committed relationship and wanted to make sure everyone I encountered knew that. So right on my desk was a picture of my wife. It was my desire to convey professionalism, courtesy, and respect. I worked at a proprietary college as an academic advisor and administrator. A part of my job was to interact with fellow administrators/counselors, instructors, and students.

My wedding ring was worn every day, and I made sure my office was open, especially when talking to women. Again, my objective was not to give the wrong impression. I think this tactic was successful. I received compliments and other nice gestures. For the most part, everything was above board. Rarely did I get someone sharing their phone number or behaving in a romantic way toward me. Mission accomplished.

Another tactic I used was to remind myself every day of my commitment as a follower of Christ and a one-woman man. I would tell myself I have many sisters but one wife. Usually, when I speak to women in a friendly manner or in a social setting, I will refer to them as Sis, short for sister. I think this term is respectful and endearing, but for me. I also use the term to remind myself of my commitment.

Infidelity is not a struggle of mine, but I am a man. So, I don't take for granted my stance or my ability to abstain from extra-marital affairs. I actively guard against it. This reminds me of a college experience.

As a senior, I received a tremendous education when I was allowed to join a twelve-step substance abuse program. The individuals and program leader were generous enough to allow someone who did not have an addiction problem to join the group as a learning assignment. I am so grateful they gave me this rare opportunity.

One of the many things I remember from this experience was People, Places, and Things. This is a mantra that those in recovery recite to themselves and each other. It is a reminder on the road of recovery to be cognizant of the People, Places, and Things associated with getting high, and to actively avoid those situations.

If you got high with certain people and they were not on the road of recovery, then you would distance yourself from them. You avoided going to the places and environments where you used to get high. Lastly, you developed better coping mechanisms to deal with life stressors or triggers acknowledging the set of circumstances that preceded the use of drugs. All these methods were used to safeguard against relapse.

I have many sisters, but one wife is a method I use along with other tactics to protect my marriage. These concepts can be used for relationships and other matters of the heart (mind). Turn a negative into a positive and be proactive to avoid situations that don't produce the outcomes you desire.

Day 362
Get it back.

Prepping a simple Sunday dinner and preparing the grill to salute the summer. Going to make some fresh lemonade and invite a family member or neighbor for dinner. Remember when family and friends gathered for Sunday dinner? Let's get it back. Be deliberate and intentional about spending quality time with those you care about.

Do you remember an activity in your past that you wished continued? If so, determine how you are going to get it back.

Day 363
Don't let people control you with their perceptions of you. Getting honest feedback and listening to others is important, but it should be developmental.

Have you ever let the perceptions others had of you alter your behavior?

_____

_____

_____

Was it a positive or negative influence? What did you learn from the experience?

_____

_____

_____

Day 364
Please read Philippians 4:4-8.

I am not sure what kind of year you've had, but I can surmise based on what happens in the world that there have been peaks and valleys, highs and lows, times of celebration, and perhaps times of mourning.

The encouragement is to think on those things that are good, noble, and true...things that are lovely, just, and pure, focusing on what is praiseworthy. Why? This mindset not only produces clarity and peace in your life, but it also builds a firm foundation of health, vigor, and vitality. This is a balanced approach with eyes wide open. You are not neglecting to acknowledge the negative or adverse experiences, as they can yield great value through learning. You are just choosing to focus your attention on that which is good. Seeing the good, admiring the good, applauding the good, reciting the good, and expecting the good.

As you enter your next year, pay close attention to those things worthy of your time and attention. Think on good things.

Day 365
Look back with thanksgiving to move forward.

Happy New Year to you and yours. It is a privilege to have an opportunity to share these thoughts with you. As you embark on your next level, let thanksgiving lead the way. Thessalonians 5:18 (NKJV) says, *"in everything give thanks; for this is the will of God in Christ Jesus for you."*

There is a power in giving thanks in all things, not for all things. You may have experienced loss due to the pandemic, illness, natural disaster, or unemployment this year. When bad things happen, it may be difficult to see a silver lining, especially when you are going through it. Whether you are in a storm of life or coming out of a storm, I pray for your strength and peace.

Look back to give thanks on your triumphs and victories. Look back to give thanks that your strength was not totally zapped, and that you made it through another year with your mind intact. If you lack the strength or feel like you can't participate in this exercise, having no energy, be grateful that others have shown you consideration, encouragement, or prayed for you. Perhaps you have not experienced any of these things. In that case, be thankful that you were able to provide comfort, support, and strength to others.

Congratulations if you accomplished everything you set out to do this year or were able to check off several items on your list. The ability to look back and honestly assess the good, bad, and ugly will enable you to learn from your experiences. Use the learning to power your upcoming year. What took you three weeks to accomplish may only take you one. Consider your mistakes and lessons they taught…this can help you make better choices moving forward.

It is my sincere desire and hope that you look back on this year with an attitude of gratitude. I hope this book helps you to enter your next level with a brighter vision and a tighter focus. I appreciate you and the opportunity you have afforded me. I am truly grateful, and I look forward to hearing your feedback about the book. Let's stay connected, sign up to get information about upcoming shows, speaking engagements, and new material at www.brothersmalls.com. Grace and Peace to you and yours.

Endnotes

[1] UMass/Dartmouth. Decision-Making Process. Retrieved from https://www.umassd.edu/fycm/decision-making/process/

[2] Former Secretary of State Tillerson, Rex. (March 22,2018). Tillerson Says Goodbye to 'a Very Mean-Spirited Town' by Gardiner Harris. Retrieved from https://www.nytimes.com/2018/03/22/us/politics/tillerson-farewell-state-department-tweet.html

[3] Bernstein, Amy. Green Carmichael, Sarah. Torres, Nicole. Opie, Tina. (January 5, 2020). Women at Work: The Challenge of Being Your True Self, An Ice Breaker on Leading with Authenticity. Retrieved from https://hbsp.harvard.edu/inspiring-minds/the-challenge-of-being-your-true-self

[4] Fay, Bill. Debt.Org.(October 19, 2021). Demographics of Debt. Retrieved from https://www.debt.org/faqs/americans-in-debt/demographics/

[5] UCSB ScienceLine. (Question Date: February 19, 2013). About how many stars are in space? Retrieved from http://scienceline.ucsb.edu/getkey.php?key=3775#:~:text=The%20number%20of%20stars%20in,stars%20in%20the%20observable%20universe!

[6] Equal Justice Institute. Retrieved from https://eji.org/about/

[7] Seltzer Ph.D., Leon F. (August 24, 2016). Self-Absorption: The Root of All (Psychological) Evil? Retrieved from https://www.psychologytoday.com/us/blog/evolution-the-self/201608/self-absorption-the-root-all-psychological-evil

[8] Rowland, Mark. Kindness Matters Guide. Retrieved from https://www.mentalhealth.org.uk/campaigns/kindness/kindness-matters-guide

[9] Wolfe, Lahle. (April 21, 2019). Learn About the Principle of Reciprocity in Business. Retrieved from https://www.thebalancesmb.com/principle-of-reciprocity-marketing-3515502

[10] Hauck, Grace. USA Today. (October 22, 2020). More than 99 million people have already voted. Here's how that compares with past elections. Retrieved from https://www.usatoday.com/story/news/politics/elections/2020/10/22/voter-turnout-2020-ranking-us-presidential-elections/6006793002/

[11] Desilver, Drew. Pew Research Center. (January 28, 2021). Turnout Soared in 2020 as nearly two-thirds of eligible U.S. voters cast ballots for president. Retrieved from https://www.pewresearch.org/fact-tank/2021/01/28/turnout-soared-in-2020-as-nearly-two-thirds-of-eligible-u-s-voters-cast-ballots-for-president/

[12] Ghose, Tia. (February 18, 2016). The Human Brain's Memory Could Store the Entire Internet. Retrieved from https://www.livescience.com/53751-brain-could-store-internet.html

[13] Watson, Traci. National Geographic News. (August 25, 2011). 86 Percent of Earth's Species Still Unknown? Retrieved from https://www.nationalgeographic.com/science/article/110824-earths-species-8-7-million-biology-planet-animals-science

[14] Wikipedia The Free Encyclopedia. Charleston Church Shooting. Retrieved from https://en.wikipedia.org/wiki/Charleston_church_shooting

[15] Doheny, Kathleen. HealthDay News. (June 16, 2016). Single Working Moms Carry a Heavy Burden. Retrieved from https://www.webmd.com/heart/news/20160616/single-working-moms-carry-a-heart-burden

[16] Rowland, Mark. Kindness Matters Guide. Retrieved from https://www.mentalhealth.org.uk/campaigns/kindness/kindness-matters-guide

[17] Van Laethem, Michelle. Beckers, Debby G.J. Van Hooff, Madelon L.M. Dijksterhuis, Ap. Geurts, Sabine A.E. Sleep Medicine, Volume 24 (2006). Day-to-day relations between stress and sleep and the mediating role of perseverative cognition. Retrieve from https://www.sciencedirect.com/science/article/abs/pii/S1389945716301113?via%3Dihub

[18] Hernandez, Rosalba. Vu, Thanh-Huyen T. Kershaw, Kiarri N. Boehm, Julia K. Kubzansky, Laura D. Carnethon, Mercedes. Trudel-Fitzgeral, Claudia. Knutson, Kristen L. Colangelo, Laura A. & Liu, Kiang (2020).The Association of Optimism with Sleep Duration and Quality: Findings from the Coronary Artery Risk and Development in Young Adults (CARDIA) Study, Behavioral Medicine, 46:2, 100-111, DOI: 10.1080/08964289.2019.1575179

[19] Koh-Hoe, Joanna, CEO of Focus on the Family Singapore. (October 28, 2016). Children need affirmation to have sense of self-security. Retrieved from https://www.todayonline.com/voices/children-need-affirmation-have-sense-self-security

[20] Primack MD PhD, Brian A., Shensa MA, Ariel., Sidani PhD MPH, James E., Whaite BS, Erin O., Lin MD, Liu yi., Rosen PHD, Daniel., Colditz MEd, Jason B., Radovic MD MSc, Ana., Miller MD PhD, Elizabeth. (March 6, 2017). Social Media Use and Perceived Social Isolation Among Young Adults in the U.S. Retrieved from https://doi.org/10.1016/j.amepre.2017.01.010

[21] Allyn, Bobby. (October 5, 2021). Here are 4 key points from the Facebook whistleblower's testimony on Capital Hill. Retrieved from https://www.npr.org/2021/10/05/1043377310/facebook-whistleblower-frances-haugen-congress

[22] Hines, Morgan. USA Today. (December 21, 2019). 'A powerhouse beauty': Rihanna mourns the loss of model and activist Mama Cax, 30. Retrieved from https://www.usatoday.com/story/entertainment/2019/12/21/rihanna-remembers-savage-x-fenty-olay-model-mama-cax-who-died-30/2720095001/

[23] Christian, Lyn. SoulSalt Inc. (August 22, 2019). The Link Between Communication Style and Success. Retrieved from https://soulsalt.com/communication-style/

[24] Princeton University. U matter. Choosing Your Communication Style. Retrieved from https://umatter.princeton.edu/respect/tools/communication-styles

[25] Garcia, Williams. (August 16, 2016). Now O'Clock: Being Mindful….it Always is.

[26] WhisperRoom Inc. (May 29,2020). 7 Benefits of Silence: Why We Need Less Noise. Retrieved from https://whisperroom.com/tips/7-benefits-of-silence-why-we-need-less-noise/

[27] Mikel, Betsy. (July 11, 2016). Neuroscience Reveals the Nourishing Benefits That Silence Has on Your Brain. Retrieved from https://www.inc.com/betsy-mikel/your-brain-benefits-most-when-you-listen-to-absolutely-nothing-science-says.html

[28] Asurion. (November 21, 2019). Americans Check Their Phones 96 Times a Day. Retrieved from https://www.asurion.com/press-releases/americans-check-their-phones-96-times-a-day/

[29] Suciu, Peter. Forbes. (June 24, 2021). Americans Spent On Average More Than 1,300 Hours On Social Media Last Year. Retrieved from https://www.forbes.com/sites/petersuciu/2021/06/24/americans-spent-more-than-1300-hours-on-social-media/?sh=315d2f852547

[30] Grover, Sam. Our Everyday Life. Emotional Effects From Having Unresolved Issues in a Relationship. Retrieved from https://oureverydaylife.com/emotional-having-unresolved-issues-relationship-8352501.html

[31] https://www.theworldcounts.com/populations/world/births

[32] https://www.youtube.com/watch?v=Q5Yol1Azjtk
www.andriennebankert.com

[33] Indeed Editorial Team. (November 19, 2020). Understanding Constructive Criticism: Definition, Tips and Examples. Retrieved from https://www.indeed.com/career-advice/career-development/constructive-criticism

Acknowledgements

I want to thank Bishop Reford Mott and Pastor Sherrie Mott for their leadership, love, counsel, and advice over the years. Bishop Jackie Wilson and Pastor Brenda Wilson, the Late Bishop Nathan S. Halton, Dr. AR Bernard, and Pastor Ray Hadjstylianos were all influential in my development and growth as a person and a believer.

Special recognition to Devon Douglass for his patient ear and honest feedback. He, along with Chauncey Hamlett, Kenneth Kweku, and Tanya Riggs provided prospective and shared insight from their professional experience and acumen.

I am grateful for the editing services rendered by Ms. Elizabeth Garrett. Thank you for sharing your skill and experience. I gained insight and understanding because of your transparency.

Lastly, I would like to thank you all in advance for the access to share my book and message with countless others. Grace and Peace.

About the Author

Omar Small built a career in municipal management on principles of communication, collaboration, coordination, and cultivation. He has held senior level positions (including Village Administrator and Deputy City Manager/HR Director) where he utilized professional relationships in the private and public sectors to address a multitude of initiatives and issues in a focused and pragmatic manner. Through thoughtful assessment and effective communication, he has managed effective teams using a direct and compassionate style.

Small served as President of the Municipal Administrators Association of Metropolitan New York. The objective of the MAA is to "strengthen the process of representative and accountable government in the New York Metropolitan Area through the promotion of professionally appointed managers and administrators." A member of the International City/County Management Association, he has shared his experience and network in the classroom, teaching graduate courses in Program Evaluation, Nonprofit and Public Management and Human Resource Management.

Small established Professional Standard Consulting to meld his professional and personal experience to provide exceptional business consulting services and products. This business aligns with his passion to help people and organizations thrive. He believes entrepreneurship can be a catalyst for dynamic positive change in communities. His new project and show, "Kicking It with Brother Smalls" at **www.brothersmalls.com** is designed to Inform, Uplift, Elevate and Inspire. Visit the site, and make sure to sign up for upcoming events, and interviews.

Small has a bachelor's degree in psychology from the University at Buffalo and a master's degree in public administration from Pace University. He also played a little football and basketball on a collegiate level and still has a pretty good cross-over ☺. Small is a gifted speaker and has been afforded opportunities to speak before various audiences in the private and public sector. He has developed mentorship programs, and shared his knowledge with young people, and those who were incarcerated.

Mr. Small is married and the privileged father of three. For more information and booking details email **info@brothersmalls.com**.

Made in the USA
Middletown, DE
14 March 2022